DIALOGUES II

European Perspectives

European Perspectives

A Series in Social Thought and Cultural Criticism

Lawrence D. Kritzman, Editor

European Perspectives presents outstanding books by leading European thinkers. With both classic and contemporary works, the series aims to shape the major intellectual controversies of our day and to facilitate the tasks of historical understanding.

For a complete list of books in the series, see pages 177–79

Dialogues II

Revised Edition

GILLES DELEUZE
and
CLAIRE PARNET

Translated by
HUGH TOMLINSON
and
BARBARA HABBERJAM

Columbia University Press
New York

Columbia University Press
Publishers Since 1893
New York   Chichester, West Sussex

Originally published in France 1977 by Flammarion, Paris
Copyright © 1977 Flammarion

English edition first published 1987
Translation, preface, and translator's introduction
copyright © 1987 The Athlone Press

Translation, preface, and translator's introduction
copyright © 2002 Continuum

Copyright © 2007 Columbia University Press

Library of Congress Cataloging-in-Publication Data
Deleuze, Gilles, 1925–1995.
    [Dialogues. English]
    Dialogues II / Gilles Deleuze and Claire Parnet; translated by Hugh
Tomlinson and Barbara Habberjam. — Rev. ed.
        p. cm. — (European perspectives)
    Includes bibliographical references and index.
    ISBN 978-0-231-14134-5 (cloth: alk. paper) — ISBN 978-0-231-14135-2
(pbk.: alk. paper)
    1. Deleuze, Gilles, 1925–1995—Interviews.   2. Philosophy.
3. Aesthetics.   4. Psychoanalysis and philosophy.   I. Parnet, Claire.
II. Title.   III. Title: Dialogues 2.   IV. Title: Dialogues two.   V. Series
B2430.D453D4313 2007
084'.1—dc22   2006031862

Casebound editions of Columbia University Press books are
printed on permanent and durable acid-free paper.

Printed in the United States of America

c   10 9 8 7 6 5 4 3 2 1
p   10 9 8 7 6 5 4 3 2 1

Contents

Preface to the English Language Edition

I have always felt that I am an empiricist, that is, a pluralist.
But what does this equivalence between empiricism and
pluralism mean? It derives from the two characteristics by
which Whitehead defined empiricism: the abstract does not
explain, but must itself be explained; and the aim is not to
rediscover the eternal or the universal, but to find the conditions under which something new is produced (*creativeness*).[1]
In so-called rationalist philosophies, the abstract is given the
task of explaining, and it is the abstract that is realized in the
concrete. One starts with abstractions such as the One, the
Whole, the Subject, and one looks for the process by which
they are embodied in a world which they make conform to
their requirements (this process can be knowledge, virtue,
history . . .). Even if it means undergoing a terrible crisis each
time that one sees rational unity or totality turning into their
opposites, or the subject generating monstrosities.

Empiricism starts with a completely different evaluation:
analysing the states of things, in such a way that non-pre-
existent concepts can be extracted from them. States of things
are neither unities nor totalities, but *multiplicities*. It is not just
that there are several states of things (each one of which would
be yet another); nor that each state of things is itself multiple
(which would simply be to indicate its resistance to unification). The essential thing, from the point of view of
empiricism, is the noun *multiplicity*, which designates a set of
lines or dimensions which are irreducible to one another.
Every 'thing' is made up in this way. Of course a multiplicity

includes focuses of unification, centres of totalization, points of subjectivation, but as factors which can prevent its growth and stop its lines. These factors are in the multiplicity to which they belong, and not the reverse. In a multiplicity what counts are not the terms or the elements, but what there is 'between', the between, a set of relations which are not separable from each other. Every multiplicity grows from the middle, like the blade of grass or the rhizome. We constantly oppose the rhizome to the tree, like two conceptions and even two very different ways of thinking. A line does not go from one point to another, but passes between the points, ceaselessly bifurcating and diverging, like one of Pollock's lines.

To extract the concepts which correspond to a multiplicity is to trace the lines of which it is made up, to determine the nature of these lines, to see how they become entangled, connect, bifurcate, avoid or fail to avoid the foci. These lines are true *becomings*, which are distinct not only from unities, but from the history in which they are developed. Multiplicities are made up of becomings without history, of individuation without subject (the way in which a river, a climate, an event, a day, an hour of the day, is individualized). That is, the concept exists just as much in empiricism as in rationalism, but it has a completely different use and a completely different nature: it is a being-multiple, instead of a being-one, a being-whole or being as subject. Empiricism is fundamentally linked to a logic – a logic of multiplicities (of which relations are only one aspect).

This book (first published in France in 1977) aims to highlight the existence and action of multiplicities in very different domains. One day Freud sensed that the psychopath experiences and thinks multiplicities: the skin is a collection of pores, the slipper, a field of stitches, the bone is extracted from an ossuary . . . But he constantly fell back on the calmer vision of a neurotic unconscious which plays with eternal abstractions (and even Melanie Klein's partial objects still refer to a unity, even if it is lost, to a totality, even if it is to come, to a subject, even if it is split). It is very difficult to reach a thought of the multiple as such, which is become noun [*substantif*] and which does not need to refer to anything other than Itself: the indefinite article as particle, the proper name as individuation without subject, the verb in the infinitive as pure becoming, 'a Hans becoming horse . . . .' It seemed to us that the great project of English and American literature was to get close to such multiplicities: it is in this literature that the question 'What is it to write?' has undoubtedly received the answer which is closest to life itself, to vegetable and animal life. It also seemed to us that the highest objective of science, mathematics and physics is multiplicity and that both set theory and the theory of spaces are still in their infancy. It seemed to us that politics is at stake as well and that in a social field rhizomes spread out everywhere under the arborescent apparatuses.

This book is made up of such a collection of musings [*rêveries*] on the formations of the unconscious, on literary, scientific and political formations.

This book itself was 'between' in several senses. It was between two books, the *Anti-Oedipus*, which Guattari and I had finished, and *A Thousand Plateaus*, which we had begun and which was our most ambitious, most immoderate and worst-received work. This book happened, therefore, not merely between two books, but between Félix Guattari and me. And as I wrote it with Claire Parnet, this was a new point which made possible a new line-between. What mattered was not the points – Félix, Claire Parnet, me and many others, who functioned simply as temporary, transitory and evanescent points of subjectivation – but the collection of bifurcating, divergent and muddled lines which constituted this book as a multiplicity and which passed between the points, carrying them along without ever going from the one to the other. Hence, the first plan for a conversation between two people, in which one asked questions and the other replied, no longer

Translators' Introduction

Dialogues was commissioned as a conventional book of interviews in a series of the same name which included interviews with writers such as Roman Jakobson and Noam Chomsky. However, as Deleuze says in the preface to this edition, it soon became clear that the 'interview' format was inappropriate: that the mechanism of 'question and answer' had the effect of forcing him into a position in which he had nothing to say. What was needed was a format in which a 'dialogue' could take place without a forced, external ordering being placed on Deleuze's thought. The result was a format in which each chapter is a 'dialogue' consisting of two halves which link and operate together in a multiplicity of ways. In the first chapter the first half is signed by Deleuze and the second by his 'interlocutor', Claire Parnet. In the other chapters the halves are unsigned and it is no longer possible to extricate the individual contributions.

The book is therefore not an 'interview' or a 'conversation' – although it has elements of both. It grows in many directions, without an overall ordering principle. To use Deleuze's terms it is the book as war-machine, the book as 'rhizome'. There is no hierarchy of root, trunk and branch, but a multiplicity of interconnected shoots going off in all directions. It is therefore both an explanation and an exemplification of 'Deleuzian pluralism'.

These 'dialogues' are themselves offshoots of Deleuze's famous seminar at the University of Vincennes (where Claire Parnet was a regular participant). This took place every

Tuesday morning, in a tiny seminar room, choked with smoke, where only those who arrived an hour early would find a seat. Deleuze's 'explorations' would be informal and far-ranging with frequent questions and interruptions. Discussions would range from Spinoza to modern music, from Chinese metallurgy to bird-song, from linguistics to gang warfare . . . The rhizome would grow, distinctions would proliferate. It was up to the participants to 'correct out' the dualisms by which Deleuze was travelling, 'to arrive at the magic formula we all seek, PLURALISM = MONISM, by passing through all the dualisms which are the enemy, the altogether necessary enemy'.[1] These processes can be seen at work here.

This book itself 'grows from the middle' of the remarkable series of works produced by Deleuze and Félix Guattari during the 1970s: *Anti-Oedipus* (1972),[2] *Kafka: Toward a Minor Literature* (1975),[3] *Rhizome* (1976)[4] and *A Thousand Plateaus* (1980).[5] Of all these works *Dialogues* is the most 'personal' and the most immediately accessible. All of them will soon be available in translation. The English-speaking reader will, for the first time, have an opportunity to form a proper assessment of a radical and original attempt to 'think' an active pluralism. Although this attempt operates against a background of a French intellectual life which is already becoming curiously dated it also has important links with English ways of thinking. These links are made explicit in the discussion of the superiority of Anglo-American literature in Chapter 2. Thus Deleuze appears from this book as an empiricist and pragmatist of a particular type: not a 'passive pragmatist' measuring things against practice but a 'constructive' pragmatist whose aim is 'the manufacture of materials to harness forces, to think the unthinkable'.[6]

We would like to thank Professor Deleuze for his assistance with the translation. We have sought to translate 'key terms' in a way which is consistent with the recent translations of all his works. We would like to thank Brian Massumi, the translator of *A Thousand Plateaus*, for his suggestions and comments.

We have followed earlier translations in rendering *agencement* as 'assemblage'.[7] The French word has both an active and a passive sense, 'a way of assembling or arranging' as well as the resulting 'ordering or arrangement'. The important term *mot d'ordre* caused us some difficulty. Its literal meaning is 'word of order' but the usual translation is 'slogan'. Professor Deleuze wanted a translation 'which highlighted the relationship to the *word* or at least to language (as in *mot de passe* [password])'. We finally decided on 'order-word'. This is also the translation independently adopted by Brian Massumi.

The French word *ritournelle* is usually translated as 'refrain' in the musical sense and also covers the repeated theme of a bird's song. After discussion with Professor Deleuze we chose the word 'ritornello' as the most appropriate English rendering. The book makes frequent use of compounds of the verb *devenir* such as *devenir-femme* or *devenir-animal*. The sense is not of something which 'becomes woman' where 'being woman' is the result of the becoming but rather of a 'pure woman becoming', without subject or object. We have therefore translated such compounds as, for example, 'woman-becoming'. This should not be interpreted as implying that something, for example 'woman', is 'becoming'. Professor Deleuze has provided a new footnote for this translation to explain his use of the term 'hecceity'.[8] We have provided some further explanations in translators' footnotes which are indicated by an asterisk (*).

We would like to thank all those who have given us advice and assistance, including Martin Joughin, Paul Patton and in particular Robert Galeta. Caroline Davidson and Richard Williams not only helped and encouraged us but had to suffer the translating process at uncomfortably close quarters.

Hugh Tomlinson
Barbara Habberjam

1

A Conversation: What is it?
What is it For?

I

It is very hard to 'explain oneself' – an interview, a dialogue, a conversation. Most of the time, when someone asks me a question, even one which relates to me, I see that, strictly, I don't have anything to say. Questions are invented, like anything else. If you aren't allowed to invent your questions, with elements from all over the place, from never mind where, if people 'pose' them to you, you haven't much to say. The art of constructing a problem is very important: you invent a problem, a problem-position, before finding a solution. None of this happens in an interview, a conversation, a discussion. Even reflection, whether it's alone, or between two or more, is not enough. Above all, not reflection. Objections are even worse. Every time someone puts an objection to me, I want to say: 'OK, OK, let's go on to something else.' Objections have never contributed anything. It's the same when I am asked a general question. The aim is not to answer questions, it's to get out, to get out of it. Many people think that it is only by going back over the question that it's possible to get out of it. 'What is the position with philosophy? Is it dead? Are we going beyond it?' It's very trying. They won't stop returning to the question in order to get out of it. But getting out never happens like that. Movement always happens behind the thinker's back, or in the moment when he blinks. Getting out is already achieved, or else it never will be. Questions are generally aimed at a future (or a past). The future of women, the future of the revolution, the future of philosophy, etc. But during this time, while you turn in circles among these questions, there are becomings which are silently at work, which are almost imperceptible. We think too much in terms of history, whether personal or universal. Becomings belong to geography, they are orientations, directions, entries and exits. There is a woman-becoming which is not the same as women, their past and their future, and it is essential that women enter this becoming to get out of their past and their future, their history. There is a revolutionary-becoming which is not the same as the future of the revolution, and which does not necessarily happen through the militants. There is a philosophy-becoming which has nothing to do with the history of philosophy and which happens through those whom the history of philosophy does not manage to classify.

To become is never to imitate, nor to 'do like', nor to conform to a model, whether it's of justice or of truth. There is no terminus from which you set out, none which you arrive at or which you ought to arrive at. Nor are there two terms which are exchanged. The question 'What are you becoming?' is particularly stupid. For as someone becomes, what he is becoming changes as much as he does himself. Becomings are not phenomena of imitation or assimilation, but of a double capture, of non-parallel evolution, of nuptials between two reigns. Nuptials are always against nature. Nuptials are the opposite of a couple. There are no longer binary machines: question–answer, masculine–feminine, man–animal, etc. This could be what a conversation is – simply the outline of a becoming. The wasp and the orchid provide the example. The orchid seems to form a wasp image, but in fact there is a wasp-becoming of the orchid, an orchid-becoming of the wasp, a double capture since 'what' each becomes changes no less than 'that which' becomes. The wasp becomes part of the orchid's reproductive apparatus at the same time as the orchid becomes the sexual organ of the wasp. One and the same becoming, a single bloc of becoming, or, as Rémy Chauvin says, an 'a-parallel evolution of two beings who have nothing whatsoever to do with one another'. There are animal-becomings of man which do not consist in playing the dog or the cat, since man and the animal only meet on the trajectory of a common but asymmetrical deterritorialization. It is like Mozart's birds: in this music there is a bird-becoming, but caught in a music-becoming of the bird, the two forming a single becoming, a single bloc, an a-parallel evolution – not an exchange, but 'a confidence with no possible interlocutor', as a commentator on Mozart says; in short, a conversation.

Becomings – they are the thing which is the most imperceptible, they are acts which can only be contained in a life and expressed in a style. Styles are not constructions, any more than are modes of life. In style it is not the words which count, nor the sentences, nor the rhythms and figures. In life it is not the stories, nor the principles, nor the consequences. You can always replace one word with another. If you don't like that one, if it doesn't suit you, take another, put another in its place. If each one of us makes this effort, everyone can understand one another and there is scarcely any reason to ask questions or to raise objections. There are no literal words, neither are there metaphors (all metaphors are sullied words, or else make them so). There are only inexact words to designate something exactly. Let us create extraordinary words, on condition that they be put to the most ordinary use and that the entity they designate be made to exist in the same way as the most common object. Today we have at our disposal new ways of reading, and perhaps of writing. There are ones which are bad and rotten. For example, we get the feeling that some books are written for the review that a journalist will have to produce, so that there is no longer even any need for a review, but only for empty words ('You must read that! It's great! Go on! You'll see!') to avoid reading the book and putting the article together. But the good ways of reading today succeed in treating a book as you would treat a record you listen to, a film or a TV programme you watch; any treatment of the book which claims for it a special respect – an attention of another kind – comes from another era and definitively condemns the book. There's no question of difficulty or understanding: concepts are exactly like sounds, colours or images, they are intensities which suit you or not, which are acceptable or aren't acceptable. Pop philosophy. There's nothing to understand, nothing to interpret. I should like to say what a style is. It belongs to people of whom you normally say, 'They have no style.' This is not a signifying structure, nor a reflected organization, nor a spontaneous inspiration, nor an orchestration, nor a little piece of music. It is an assemblage, an assemblage of enunciation. A style is managing to stammer in one's own language. It is difficult, because there has to be a need for such stammering. Not being a stammerer in one's speech, but being a stammerer of language itself. Being like a foreigner in one's own language. Constructing a line of flight. The most striking examples for me are Kafka, Beckett, Gherasim Luca and Godard. Gherasim Luca is a great poet among the greatest: he invented a prodigious stammering, his own. He gave public readings of his poems in front of two hundred people; and yet it was an event, an event belonging to no school or movement, which would pass through these two hundred. Things never pass where you think, nor along the paths you think.

You can always object that we are choosing favourable examples, Kafka the Czech Jew writing in German, the Irish Beckett writing English and French, Luca, of Rumanian origin, and even the Swiss Godard. And so? This is not the problem for any of them. We must be bilingual even in a single language, we must have a minor language inside our own languge, we must create a minor use of our own language. Multilingualism is not merely the property of several systems each of which would be homogeneous in itself: it is primarily the line of flight or of variation which affects each system by stopping it from being homogeneous. Not speaking like an Irishman or a Rumanian in a language other than one's own, but on the contrary speaking in one's own language like a foreigner. Proust says: 'Great literature is written in a sort of foreign language. To each sentence we attach a meaning, or at any rate a mental image, which is often a mistranslation. But in great literature all our mistranslations result in beauty.'[1] This is the good way to read: all mistranslations are good – always provided that they do not consist in interpretations, but relate to the use of the book, that they multiply its use, that they create yet another language inside its language. 'Great literature is written in a sort of foreign language . . .' That is the definition of style. Here again it is a question of becoming. People always think of a majoritarian future (when I am grown up, when I have power). Whereas the problem is that of a minoritarian-becoming, not pretending, not playing or imitating the child, the madman, the woman, the animal, the stammerer or the foreigner, but becoming all these, in order to invent new forces or new weapons.

Life is like that too. In life there is a sort of awkwardness, a delicacy of health, a frailty of constitution, a vital stammering which is someone's charm. Charm is the source of life just as style is the source of writing. Life is not your history – those who have no charm have no life, it is as though they are dead. But the charm is not the person. It is what makes people be grasped as so many combinations and so many unique chances from which such a combination has been drawn. It is a throw of the dice which necessarily wins, since it affirms chance sufficiently instead of detaching or mutilating chance or reducing it to probabilities. Thus through each fragile combination a power of life is affirmed with a strength, an obstinacy, an unequalled persistence in the being. It is strange how great thinkers have a fragile personal life, an uncertain health, at the same time as they carry life to the state of absolute power or of 'Great Health'. These are not people, but the figure of their own combination. Charm and style are poor words; we should find others, replace them. Charm gives life a non-personal power, above individuals; at the same time, style gives writing an external end [*fin*] – which goes beyond what is written. And this is the same thing: writing does not have its end in itself precisely because life is not something personal. The only aim [*fin*] of writing is life, through the combinations which it draws. This is the opposite of 'neurosis', in which life is constantly mutilated, debased, personalized, mortified, and in which writing takes itself as its own end. Nietzsche, the opposite of the neurotic, very much alive but with fragile health, writes:

> It sometimes seems as though the artist, and the philosopher in particular, is only a chance in his time . . . nature, which never makes a leap, has made its one leap in creating them, and a leap of joy moreover, for nature then feels that for the first time it has reached its goal – where it realises it has to unlearn having goals and that it has played the game of life and becoming with too high stakes. This knowledge transfigures nature, and a gentle eve-ning-weariness, that which men call 'beauty', reposes upon its face.[2]

When you work, you are necessarily in absolute solitude. You cannot have disciples, or be part of a school. The only work is moonlighting and is clandestine. But it is an extremely populous solitude. Populated not with dreams, phantasms or plans, but with encounters. An encounter is perhaps the same thing as a becoming, or nuptials. It is from the depth of this solitude that you can make any encounter whatsoever. You encounter people (and sometimes without knowing them or ever having seen them) but also movements, ideas, events, entities. All these things have proper names, but the proper name does not designate a person or a subject. It designates an effect, a zigzag, something which passes or happens be-tween two as though under a potential difference: the 'Compton effect', the 'Kelvin effect'. We said the same thing about becomings: it is not one term which becomes the other, but each encounters the other, a single becoming which is not common to the two, since they have nothing to do with one another, but which is between the two, which has its own direction, a bloc of becoming, an a-parallel evolution. This is it, the double capture, the wasp AND the orchid: not even something which would be in the one, or something which would be in the other, even if it had to be exchanged, be mingled, but something which is between the two, outside the two, and which flows in another direction. To encounter is to find, to capture, to steal, but there is no method for finding other than a long preparation. Stealing is the opposite of plagiarizing, copying, imitating, or doing like. Capture is always a double-capture, theft a double-theft, and it is that which creates not something mutual, but an asymmetrical block, an a-parallel evolution, nuptials, always 'outside' and 'between'. So this is what it would be, a conversation.

> Yes, I am a thief of thoughts
> not, I pray, a stealer of souls
> I have built an' rebuilt
> upon what is waitin'
> for the sand on the beaches
> carves many castles
> on what has been opened
> before my time
> a word, a tune, a story, a line
> keys in the wind t'unlock my mind
> an' t'grant my closet thoughts backyard air
> it is not of me t'sit an' ponder
> wonderin' an' wastin' time
> thinkin' of thoughts that haven't been thunk
> thinkin' of dreams that haven't been dreamt
> an' new ideas that haven't been wrote
> an' new words t'fit into rhyme [. . .]
> an' not t'worry about the new rules
> for they ain't been made yet

an' t'shout my singin' mind
knowin' that it is me an' my kind
that will make those rules . . .
if the people of tomorrow
really need the rules of today
rally 'round all you prosecutin' attorneys
the world is but a courtroom
yes
but I know the defendants better 'n you
and while you're busy prosecutin'
we're busy whistlin'
cleanin' up the courtroom
sweepin' sweepin'
listenin' listenin'
winkin' t'one another
careful
    careful
your spot is comin' up soon.[3]

How proud and wonderful – also modest – is this Bob Dylan poem. It says it all. As a teacher I should like to be able to give a course as Dylan organizes a song, as astonishing producer rather than author. And that it should begin as he does, suddenly, with his clown's mask, with a technique of contriving, and yet improvising each detail. The opposite of a plagiarist, but also the opposite of a master or a model. A very lengthy preparation, yet no method, nor rules, nor recipes. Nuptials without couples or conjugality. Having a bag into which I put everything I encounter, provided that I am also put in a bag. Finding, encountering, stealing instead of regulating, recognizing and judging. For recognizing is the opposite of the encounter. Judging is the profession of many people, and it is not a good profession, but it is also the use to which many people put writing. Better to be a road-sweeper than a judge. The more one has been fooled in one's life, the more one gives lessons: no one is as good as a Stalinist in

giving lessons in non-Stalinism and pronouncing 'new rules'.
There is a whole race of judges, and the history of thought is
like that of a court, it lays claim to a court of Pure Reason, or
else Pure Faith . . . This is why people speak so readily in the
name and in the place of others, and why they like questions
so much, are so clever at asking them and replying to them.
There are also those who demand to be judged, if only to be
recognized as guilty. In justice they demand conformity, even
if this is to rules which they invent, to a transcendence which
they claim to reveal or to feelings which motivate them.
Justice and correctness are bad ideas. Compare Godard's
formula; not a correct image, just an image [*pas une image juste,
juste une image*]. It is the same in philosophy as in a film or a
song: no correct ideas, just ideas [*pas d'idées justes, justes des
idées*]. Just ideas: this is the encounter, the becoming, the theft
and the nuptials, this 'between-two' of solitudes. When
Godard says he would like to be a production studio, he is
obviously not trying to say that he wants to produce his own
films or he wants to edit his own books. He is trying to say just
ideas, because, when it comes down to it, you are all alone,
and yet you are like a conspiracy of criminals. You are no
longer an author, you are a production studio, you have never
been more populated. Being a 'gang' – gangs live through the
worst dangers; forming judges, courts, schools, families and
conjugalities again. But what is good in a gang, in principle, is
that each goes about his own business while encountering
others, each brings in his loot and a becoming is sketched out
– a bloc starts moving – which no longer belongs to anyone,
but is 'between' everyone, like a little boat which children let
slip and lose, and is stolen by others. In the TV conversations
6 times 2 what were Godard and Mieville doing if not making
the richest use of their solitude, using it as a means of encounter, making a line or bloc shoot between two people,
producing all the phenomena of a double capture, showing
what the conjunction AND is, neither a union, nor a
juxtaposition, but the birth of a stammering, the outline of a

broken line which always sets off at right angles, a sort of active and creative line of flight? AND . . . AND . . . AND . . .

You should not try to find whether an idea is just or correct. You should look for a completely different idea, elsewhere, in another area, so that something passes between the two which is neither in one nor the other. Now, one does not generally find this idea alone; a chance is needed, or else someone gives you one. You don't have to be learned, to know or be familiar with a particular area, but to pick up this or that in areas which are very different. This is better than the 'cut-up'. It is rather a 'pick-me-up or 'pick-up'^{4*} – in the dictionary = collecting up, chance, restarting of the motor, getting on to the wavelength; and then the sexual connotation of the word. Burroughs' cut-up is still a method of probabilities – at least linguistic ones – and not a procedure of drawing lots or a single chance which combines the heterogeneous elements. For example, I am trying to explain that things, people, are made up of very varied lines, and that they do not necessarily know which line they are on or where they should make the line which they are tracing pass; in short, there is a whole geography in people, with rigid lines, supple lines, lines of flight, etc. I see my friend Jean-Pierre, who explains to me, in connection with something else, that a monetary balance implies a line between two sorts of operations which are apparently simple: but in fact economists can make this line pass anywhere, so that they haven't the slightest idea where to make it pass. This is an encounter, but with whom? With Jean-Pierre, with a field, with a word, with a gesture? I always worked in this way with Fanny. Her ideas always seized me from behind, coming from far away in another direction, so that we crossed all the more like the signals from two lamps. In her own work, she came upon Lawrence's poems about tortoises. I do not know anything about tortoises and yet that changes everything for animal-becomings; it is not clear that any animal whatsoever is caught up in these becomings; what about tortoises or giraffes? Lawrence says: 'If I am a giraffe and the English people who write about me are well-trained dogs, nothing works any more, the animals are too different. You say that you like me, but believe me, you don't like me, you instinctively detest the animal that I am.' Our enemies are dogs. But what precisely is an encounter with someone you like? Is it an encounter with someone, or with the animals who come to populate you, or with the ideas which take you over, the movements which move you, the sounds which run through you? And how do you separate these things? I can talk of Foucault, tell you that he has said this or that to me, set it out as I see it. This is nothing as long as I have not been able really to encounter this set of sounds hammered out, of decisive gestures, of ideas all made of tinder and fire, of deep attention and sudden closure, of laughter and smiles which one feels to be 'dangerous' at the very moment when one feels tenderness – this set as a unique combination whose proper name would be Foucault. A man without references, says François Ewald – the finest compliment . . . Jean-Pierre, the only friend whom I have never left and who has never left me . . . And Jerome, that silhouette, always walking, moving, penetrated to the core with life, and whose generosity, love, was nourished at a secret source, JONAH . . . In each of us there is, as it were, an ascesis, in part turned against ourselves. We are deserts, but populated by tribes, flora and fauna. We pass out time in ordering these tribes, arranging them in other ways, getting rid of some and encouraging others to prosper. And all these clans, all these crowds, do not undermine the desert, which is our very ascesis; on the contrary they inhabit it, they pass through it, over it. In Guattari there has always been a sort of wild rodeo, in part directed against himself. The desert, experimentation on oneself, is our only identity, our single chance for all the combinations which inhabit us. Then we are told, 'You are not masters, but you are even more suffocating.' We should have so much liked to be something else.

I was taught by two professors, whom I liked and admired a lot, Alquié and Hyppolite. Everything turned out badly. One had long white hands and a stammer which might have been a legacy of childhood, or there to hide a native accent, and which was harnessed to the service of Cartesian dualisms. The other had a powerful face with unfinished features, and rhythmically beat out Hegelian triads with his fist, hanging his words on the beats. At the Liberation we were still strangely stuck in the history of philosophy. We simply plunged into Hegel, Husserl and Heidegger; we threw ourselves like puppies into a scholasticism worse than that of the Middle Ages. Fortunately there was Sartre. Sartre was our Outside, he was really the breath of fresh air from the backyard (and it was of little importance to know exactly what his relationship with Heidegger was, from the point of view of a history to come). Among all the Sorbonne's probabilities, it was his unique combination which gave us the strength to tolerate the new restoration of order. And Sartre has never stopped being that, not a model, a method or an example, but a little fresh air – a gust of air even when he had just been to the Café Flore – an intellectual who singularly changed the situation of the intellectual. It is idiotic to wonder whether Sartre was the beginning or the end of something. Like all creative things and people, he is in the middle, he grows from the middle. However, at that time I did not feel drawn towards existentialism or towards phenomenology; I am not quite sure why, but it was already history when you got there, too much method, imitation, commentary and interpretation – except Sartre. So, after the Liberation, the history of philosophy tightened itself around us – without our realizing it – under the pretext of opening up a future of thought, which would also be the most ancient thought. The 'Heidegger question' did not seem to me to be 'Is he a bit of a Nazi?' (obviously, obviously) but 'What was his rôle in this new injection of history of philosophy?' No one takes thought very seriously, except those who claim to be thinkers or philosophers by profession. But that doesn't stop it from having its own apparatuses of power – or its being an effect of its apparatus of power when it tells people: 'Don't take me seriously, because I think for you, since I give you conformity, norms and rules, an image'; to all of which you may submit all the more as you say: 'That's not my business, it's not important, it's for philosophers and their pure theories.' The history of philosophy has always been the agent of power in philosophy, and even in thought. It has played the represser's role: how can you think without having read Plato, Descartes, Kant and Heidegger, and so-and-so's book about them? A formidable school of intimidation which manufactures specialists in thought – but which also makes those who stay outside conform all the more to this specialism which they despise. An image of thought called philosophy has been formed historically and it effectively stops people from thinking. Philosophy's relationship with the State is not solely due to the fact that recently most philosophers have been 'public professors'[5*] (although this fact has had a very different significance in France and Germany). The relationship goes further back. For thought borrows its properly philosophical image from the state as beautiful, substantial or subjective interiority. It invents a properly spiritual State, as an absolute state, which is by no means a dream, since it operates effectively in the mind. Hence the importance of notions such as universality, method, question and answer, judgement, or recognition, of just correct, always having correct ideas. Hence the importance of themes like those of a republic of spirits, an enquiry of the understanding, a court of reason, a pure 'right' of thought, with ministers of the Interior and bureaucrats of pure thought. Philosophy is shot through with the project of becoming the official language of a Pure State. The exercise of thought thus conforms to the goals of the real State, to the dominant meanings and to the requirements of the established order. Nietzsche said everything on this point in 'Schopenhauer Educator'.[6*] Everything which belongs to a thought without image – nomadism, the war-machine, becomings, nuptials against nature, capture and thefts, interregnums, minor languages or stammering of language, etc. – is crushed and denounced as a nuisance. Of course, this role of represser of thought can be played by disciplines other than philosophy and its history. It can even be said that today the history of philosophy has gone bankrupt and that 'the State no longer needs the sanction of Philosophy'. But keen competitors have already taken its place. Epistemology has taken up the reins from the history of philosophy. Marxism brandishes a judgement of history, or even a people's tribunal – which are even more disturbing than the others. Psychoanalysis increasingly concerns itself with the 'thought' function and – not without reason – allies itself with linguistics. These are the new apparatuses of power in thought itself, and Marx, Freud and Saussure make up a strange, three-headed Represser, a dominant major language. To interpret, to transform, to utter are the new forms of 'correct' ideas. Even Chomsky's syntactic marker is primarily a marker of power. Linguistics triumphed at the same time as information was being developed as power, and was imposing its image of language and of thought, consistent with the transmission of 'order-words'[7]* and the organization of re-dundancies. There is not really much point in wondering whether philosophy is dead, when many other disciplines are assuming its function. We have no right to lay claim to madness, since madness itself passes through psychoanalysis and linguistics reunited, since it is imbued with correct ideas, with a strong culture or a history without becoming, since it has its clowns, its professors and its little chiefs.

So I began with the history of philosophy – when it was still being prescribed. For my part, I could not see any way of extracting myself. I could not stand Descartes, the dualisms and the Cogito, or Hegel, the triad and the operation of the negation. But I liked writers who seemed to be part of the history of philosophy, but who escaped from it in one respect,

or altogether: Lucretius, Spinoza, Hume, Nietzsche, Bergson.
Of course, every history of philosophy has its chapter on
empiricism: Locke and Berkeley have their place there, but in
Hume there is something very strange which completely dis-
places empiricism, giving it a new power, a theory and
practice of relations, of the AND, which was to be pursued by
Russell and Whitehead, but which remains underground or
marginal in relation to the great classifications, even when
they inspire a new conception of logic and epistemology.
Bergson, of course, was also caught up in French-style history
of philosophy, and yet in him there is something which cannot
be assimilated, which enabled him to provide a shock, to be a
rallying point for all the opposition, the object of so many
hatreds: and this is not so much because of the theme of
duration, as of the theory and practice of becomings of all
kinds, of coexistent multiplicities. And it is easy to credit
Spinoza with the place of honour in the Cartesian succession;
except that he bulges out of that place in all directions, there is
no living corpse who raises the lid of his coffin so powerfully,
crying so loudly 'I am not one of yours.' It was on Spinoza
that I worked the most seriously according to the norms of the
history of philosophy – but he more than any other gave me
the feeling of a gust of air from behind each time you read him,
of a witch's broom which he makes you mount. We have not
yet begun to understand Spinoza, and I myself no more than
others. All these thinkers are of a fragile constitution, and yet
shot through with an unsurmountable life. They proceed only
through positive and affirmative force. They have a sort of cult
life (I fantasize about writing a memorandum to the Academy
of the Moral Sciences to show that Lucretius' book cannot end
with the description of the plague, and that it is an invention,
a falsification of the Christians who wanted to show that a
maleficent thinker *must* end in terror and anguish). These
thinkers have few relationships with each other – apart from
Nietzsche and Spinoza – and yet they do have them. One
might say that something happens between them, at different

neither is it enough to say, 'Down with genres'; one must effectively write in such a way that there are no more 'genres', etc.) With Félix, all that became possible, even if we failed. We were only two, but what was important for us was less our working together than this strange fact of working between the two of us. We stopped being 'author'. And these 'between-the-twos' referred back to other people, who were different on one side from on the other. The desert expanded, but in so doing became more populous. This had nothing to do with a school, with processes of recognition, but much to do with encounters. And all these stories of becomings, of nuptials against nature, of a-parallel evolution, of bilingualism, of theft of thoughts, were what I had with Félix. I stole Félix, and I hope he did the same for me. You know how we work – I repeat it because it seems to me to be important – we do not work together, we work between the two. In these conditions, as soon as there is this type of multiplicity, there is politics, micro-politics. As Félix says: before Being there is politics. We don't work, we negotiate. We were never in the same rhythm, we were always out of step: I understood and could make use of what Félix said to me six months later; he understood what I said to him immediately, too quickly for my liking – he was already elsewhere. From time to time we have written about the same idea, and have noticed later that we have not grasped it at all in the same way: witness 'bodies without organs'. Or take another example. Félix was working on black holes; this astronomical idea fascinated him. The black hole is what captures you and does not let you get out. How do you get out of a black hole? How do you transmit signals from the bottom of a black hole? I was working, rather, on a white wall: what is a white wall, a screen, how do you plane down the wall and make a line of flight pass? We had not brought the two ideas together, but we noticed that each was tending of its own accord towards the other, to produce something which, in-deed, was neither in the one nor the other. For black holes on a white wall are in fact a face, a broad face with white cheeks, and pierced with black holes. Now it no longer seems like a face, it is rather the assemblage or the abstract machine which is to produce the face. Suddenly the problem bounces back and it is political: what are the societies, the civilizations which need to make this machine work, that is, to produce, to 'overcode' the whole body and head with a face, and to what end? It is not obvious, the beloved's face, the boss's face, the faceification of the physical and social body . . . Here is a multiplicity with at least three dimensions, astronomical, aesthetic, political. In none of the cases are we making a metaphorical use of it: we don't say that is 'like' black holes in astronomy, that is 'like' a white canvas in painting. We are using deterritorialized terms, that is, terms which are torn from their area, in order to reterritorialize another notion, the 'face', 'faceity' as social function. And, still worse, people keep on being sunk in black holes, pinioned on a white wall. This is what being identified, labelled, recognized is: a central computer functioning as a black hole and sweeping across a white wall without contours. We are talking literally. In fact, astronomers envisage the possibility that, in the centre of a globular cluster, all sorts of black holes will converge to form a single hole of a fairly large mass . . . White wall – black hole: this, for me, is a typical example of the way in which a work is assembled betwen us, neither union nor juxtaposition, but a broken line which shoots between two, proliferation, tentacles.

This is a pick-up[8*] method. No, 'method' is a bad word. But pick-up as procedure is Fanny's word. Her only fear was that it was too much of a pun. Pick-up is a stammering. It is only valid in opposition to Burroughs' cut-up: there is no cutting, folding and turning down, but multiplications according to the growing dimensions. The pick-up or the double theft, the a-parallel evolution, does not happen between persons, it happens between ideas, each one being deterritorialized in the other, following a line or lines which are neither in one nor the other, and which carry off a 'bloc'. I do not wish to reflect on what is past. At present, Félix and I are finishing a large book.

It is nearly finished, and it will be the last. Afterwards we will see. We will do something else. I should therefore like to talk about what we are doing now. There is not one of these ideas which did not come from Félix, from Félix's side (black hole, micro-politics, deterritorialization, abstract machine, etc.). Now is the moment to exercise the method, or never: you and I, we can make use of it in another bloc or on another side, with your own ideas, so that something is produced which doesn't belong to either of us, but is between 2, 3, 4 . . . n. No longer is it 'x explains x, signed x', but 'Deleuze explains Guattari, signed you', 'x explains y, signed z'. Thus the conversation would become a real function. 'On the side of'[9*] . . . One must multiply the sides, break every circle in favour of the polygons.

G.D.

II

If the question and answer procedure is not suitable it's for very simple reasons. The tone of questions can vary: there is a clever/treacherous tone, or on the contrary, a servile tone, or again, an equal-to-equal tone. You hear them every day on television. But it is always like the Luca poem (I don't quote exactly): Shooters and shot . . . front to front . . . back to back . . . front to back . . . back to back and to front. Whatever the tone, the process of question and answer is made to nourish dualisms. For example, in a literary interview, there is first of all the interviewer/interviewee dualism, and then, beyond, the man/writer, life/work dualisms in the interviewee himself, and again, the dualism between the work and the intention or the meaning of the work. And when it's a colloquium or a round table it's the same. Dualisms no longer relate to unities, but to successive choices: are you white or black, man or woman, rich or poor, etc.? Do you take the left half or the right half? There is always a binary machine which governs the distribution of roles and which means that all the answers must go through preformed questions, since the questions are already worked out on the basis of the answers assumed to be probable according to the dominant meanings. Thus a grille is constituted such that everything which does not pass through the grille cannot be materially understood. For example, in a broadcast on prisons the following choices will be established: jurist/prison governor, judge/lawyer, social worker/interesting case, the opinion of the ordinary prisoners who fill the prisons being pushed back outside the grille or outside the subject. It is in this sense that we are always 'had' by television, we have lost in advance. Even when we are speaking for ourselves, we always speak in the place of someone else who will not be able to speak.

You cannot escape being had, possessed or rather dispossessed. Consider the well-known card trick, 'forced choice'. You want to make someone choose, for example, the king of hearts. You say first of all: 'Do you prefer red or black?' If he answers 'Red', you withdraw the black cards from the table; if he replies 'Black', you take the red cards and again you withdraw them. You have only to continue: 'Do you prefer hearts or diamonds?' Until 'Do you prefer the king or the queen of hearts?' The binary machine works in this way, even when the interviewer is a person of good will. The point is that the machine goes beyond us and serves other ends. Psychoanalysis is exemplary in this respect, with its process of the association of ideas. I swear that the examples that I give are real, although confidential and non-personal. (1) A patient says, 'I want to go off with a hippy group' [*groupe hippie*], the manipulator replies, 'Why do you say big pee?' [*gros pipi*]. (2) A patient speaks of the Bouches du Rhône, the psychoanalyst himself comments, 'Invitation to a journey that I emphasize with a mother's mouth' (if you say 'mother' [*mère*] I keep it and if you say 'sea' [*mer*] I withdraw it, thus I win at each move). (3) A depressed patient speaks of his memories of the Resistance and of a chief of the network called René. The psychoanalyst says, 'Let us keep René.' *Re-né* [reborn] is no longer Resistance, it's Renaissance. And Renaissance, is it François I or the mother's womb? Let us keep 'mother'. Oh yes, psychoanalysis is not at all the purloined letter, it is the forced choice. Where it commands attention, it is because it gave the binary machine new material and a new extension, consistent with what we expect of an apparatus of power. Where it does not command attention it is because there were other means. Psychoanalysis is a very cold enterprise (a culture of death drives and of castration, of the dirty 'little secret') to crush all the patient's utterances, to retain only their anaemic double, and to push outside the grid all that the patient has said about his desires, his experiences and his assemblages, his politics, his loves and his hates. There were already so many people, so many priests, so many representatives who spoke in the name of our conscience, it was necessary for this race of priests and representatives to speak in the name of the unconscious.

It is wrong to say that the binary machine exists only for reasons of convenience. It is said that 'the base 2' is the easiest. But in fact the binary machine is an important component of apparatuses of power. So many dichotomies will be established that there will be enough for everyone to be pinned to the wall, sunk in a hole. Even the divergences of deviancy will be measured according to the degree of binary choice; you are neither white nor black, Arab then? Or halfbreed? You are neither man nor woman, transvestite then? This is the white wall/black hole system. And it is not surprising that the face has such importance in this system: you must have the face of your role – in such and such a place among the possible elementary unities, on such and such a level in the possible successive choices. Nothing is less personal than the face. Even the madman must have a face corresponding to some type which we expect of him. When a schoolteacher has a strange appearance, we are at this last level of choice, and we say: yes, it is the schoolteacher, but, look she is depressed, or she has gone mad. The base model, first level, is the face of the ordinary European of today – what Ezra Pound calls the ordinary sensual man, Ulysses. All types of face will be determined on the basis of this model, through successive dichotomies. If linguistics itself proceeds by dichotomies (cf. Chomsky's trees where a binary machine works inside language), if informatics proceeds through the succession of dual choices, this is not so innocent as one might think. It is perhaps that information is a myth and that language is not essentially informative. First of all there is a language-face relationship, and, as Félix says, language is always indexed on features of the face, features of 'faceicity': 'Look at me when I speak to you . . .' or 'Lower your eyes . . . What? What did you say, why do you look so glum?' What the linguists call 'distinctive features' would not even be discernible without the features of faceicity. And it is all the more obvious that language is not neutral, not informative. Language is not made to be believed but to be obeyed. When the schoolteacher explains an operation to the children, or when she teaches them grammar, she does not, strictly speaking, give them information, she communicates orders to them, she transmits 'order-words' to them, necessarily conforming to dominant meanings. This is why it would be necessary to modify the schemea of informatics. The schema of informatics begins from a presumed maximal theoretical information; at the other end, it puts noise as interference, anti-information and, between the two, redundancy, which diminishes theoretical information but also enables it to overcome noise. On the contrary, this would be: above, redundancy as mode of existence and of propagation of orders (the newspapers, the 'news', proceed by redundancy); underneath, the face-information, as always the minimum required for the comprehension of orders; and lower still, something which could be either the shout, or silence, or stuttering, and which would be like language's line of flight, speaking in one's own language as a foreigner, making a minority use of language. One could also say: undo the face, unravel the face. Anyway, if linguistics, if informatics, play a repressive role today, it is because they themselves function as binary machines in these apparatuses of power and constitute a whole formalization of order rather than a pure science of units of language and of abstract information contents.

In everything you have written there is the theme of an image of thought which would impede thinking, which would impede the exercise of thought. Nevertheless, you are not a Heideggerian. You love the grass rather than the trees and the forest. You do not say that we are not yet thinking, and that there is a future of thought which plunges into the most immemorial past, and that, between the two, everything would be 'hidden from view'. Future and past don't have much meaning, what counts is the present-becoming: geography and not history, the middle and not the beginning or the end, grass which is in the middle and which grows from the middle, and not trees which have a top and roots. Always grass between the paving stones. But it is thought which is crushed by these paving stones which are called philosophy, by these images which suffocate and jaundice it. 'Images' here doesn't refer to ideology but to a whole organization which effectively trains thought to operate according to the norms of an established order or power, and moreover, installs in it an apparatus of power, sets it up as an apparatus of power itself. The Ratio as tribunal, as universal State, as republic of spirits (the more you are subjected, the more you are legislators, for you are only subject . . . to pure reason). In *Différence et Ré-pétition*, [10*]) you tried to enumerate these images which offer autonomous ends to thought, in order to make it serve ends which can hardly be acknowledged. They can all be summarized in the order-word: have correct ideas! It is first of all the image of good nature and good will – good will of the thinker who seeks the 'truth', good nature of thought which possesses 'the true' by right. Then, it is the image of a 'common sense' – harmony of all the faculties of a thinking being. Then, again, it is the image of recognition – 'to recognize', doesn't this mean that something or someone is set up as a model of the activities of the thinker who makes use of all his faculties on an object which is supposedly the same. Then again, it is the image of error – as if thought had only to mistrust external influences capable of making it take the 'false' as true. Finally, it is the image of knowledge – as place of truth, and truth as sanctioning answers or solutions for questions and problems which are supposedly 'given'.

The interesting point is just as much the reverse: how can thought shake off its model, make its grass grow – even locally, even at the margins, imperceptibly. Thoughts: (1) which would not originate in a good nature and a good will, but which would come from a violence suffered by thought; (2) which do not operate in a concord of faculties, but which, on the contrary, would take each faculty to the limit of its discordance with the others; (3) which would not be closed on recognition, but which would open to encounters and would always be defined as a function of an Outside; (4) which would not have to struggle against error, but would have to disengage themselves from a more internal and more powerful enemy, stupidity; (5) which would be defined in the movement of learning and not in the result of knowledge, and which would not leave it to anyone, to any Power, to 'pose' questions or to 'set' problems. And even authors about whom you have written, whether it is Hume, Spinoza, Nietzsche or Proust, or whether it is Foucault – you did not treat them as authors, that is as objects of recognition, you found in them these acts of thought without image, blind as well as blinding, these violences, these encounters, these nuptials which make them creators well before they are authors. It can always be said that you were trying to pull them towards you. But they would scarcely let themselves be pulled. You would only meet those who had not been waiting for you to produce encounters in themselves, you claimed to extricate from the history of philosophy those who had not waited for you in order to emerge. You only found creators in those in who had not waited for you in order to stop being authors (neither Spinoza nor Nietzsche were 'authors': they escape from it, the one by the power of a geometrical method, the other by aphorisms which are the opposite of an author's maxims; even Proust escapes, by the game of the narrator; and Foucault, cf. the ways he suggests for escaping the function of the author in *L'Ordre du Discours*[11*]). At the same time that an author is designated, thought is subjected to an image and writing is made an activity different from life, having its ends in itself . . . in order better to serve ends against life.

Your work with Félix (writing *à deux* is already a way of stopping being an author) has not got you out of this problem but has given it a very different orientation. You set about opposing the rhizome to trees. And trees are not a metaphor at all, but an image of thought, a functioning, a whole apparatus that is planted in thought in order to make it go in a straight line and produce the famous correct ideas. There are all kinds of characteristics in the tree: there is a point of origin, seed or centre; it is a binary machine or principle of dichotomy, with its perpetually divided and reproduced branchings, its points of arborescence; it is an axis of rotation which organizes things in a circle, and the circles round the centre; it is a structure, a system of points and positions which fix all of the possible within a grid; a hierarchical system or transmission of orders, with a central instance and recapitulative memory; it has a future and a past, roots and a peak, a whole history, an evolution, a development; it can be cut up by cuts which are said to be significant in so far as they follow its arborescences, its branchings, its concentricities, its moments of development. Now, there is no doubt that trees are planted in our heads: the tree of life, the tree of knowledge, etc. The whole world demands roots. Power is always arborescent. There are few disciplines which do not go through schemas of arborescence: biology, linguistics, informatics (automata or

centred systems). And yet, nothing goes through there, even
in these disciplines. Each decisive act testifies to another
thought, in so far as thoughts are things themselves. There are
multiplicities which constantly go beyond binary machines
and do not let themselves be dichotomized. There are centres
everywhere, like multiplicities of black holes which do not let
themselves be agglomerated. There are lines which do not
amount to the path of a point, which break free from structure
– lines of flight, becomings, without future or past, without
memory, which resist the binary machine – woman-becoming
which is neither man nor woman, animal-becoming which is
neither beast nor man. Non-parallel evolutions, which do not
proceed by differentiation, but which leap from one line to
another, between completely heterogeneous beings; cracks,
imperceptible ruptures, which break the lines even if they
resume elsewhere, leaping over significant breaks . . . The
rhizome is all this. Thinking in things, among things – this is
producing a rhizome and not a root, producing the line and
not the point. Producing population in a desert and not
species and genres in a forest. Populating without ever
specifying.

What is the situation today? For a long time literature and
even the arts have been organized into 'schools'. Schools are of
the arborescent type. And a school is already terrible: there is
always a pope, manifestos, representatives, declarations of
avant-gardeism, tribunals, excommunications, impudent
political volte-faces, etc. The worst thing about schools is not
merely the sterilization of disciples (they have richly deserved
it), it is rather the crushing, the suffocation, of all that
happened before or at the same time – as 'Symbolism'
suffocated the extraordinarily rich poetic movement of the late
nineteenth century, as Surrealism crushed the international
Dadaist movement, etc. Today schools are no longer fee-
paying, but operate for the benefit of a still darker organization: a kind of marketing, where the interest has moved and
no longer relates to books but to newspaper articles,

broadcasts, debates, colloquia, round tables about a doubtful book which, at the limit, doesn't even need to exist. Is this the death of the book as McLuhan predicted? There is a very complex phenomenon here: the cinema above all, but also to a certain extent the newspapers, the radio and the TV, have themselves been powerful elements which have brought the author-function into question and have released creative functions – at least potentially – which no longer pass through an Author.

But as writing taught itself to detach itself from the author-function, it has been reconstituted at the periphery, regaining credit on the radio, the TV, in the newspapers, and even in the cinema (the *cinéma d'auteur*). At the same time as journalism has increasingly created the events about which it speaks, the journalist has discovered himself to be an author and has given reality back to a function which had fallen into discredit. The relationships of force between press and book have changed completely and writers or intellectuals have passed into the service of journalists, or become their own journalists, journalists of themselves. They have become the servants of interviewers, debaters, and presenters: the journalization of the writer, clown's tricks that the radios and TVs make the consenting writers undergo. André Scala has anlysed this new situation very well. Hence the possibility of marketing which is today replacing the old-fashioned schools. So that the problem consists in reinventing – not simply for writing, but also for the cinema, the radio, the TV, and even for journalism – the creative or productive functions freed of this always reappearing author-function. For the dis-advantages of the Author are constituting a point of departure or of origin, forming a subject of enunciation on which all the produced utterances depend, getting recognized and identified in an order of dominant meanings or established powers: 'I in my capacity as . . .' Creative functions are com-pletely different, nonconformist usages of the rhizome and not the tree type, which proceed by intersections, crossings of lines, points of encounter in the middle: there is no subject, but instead collective assemblages of enunciation; there are no specificities but instead populations, music-writing-sciences-audio-visual, with their relays, their echoes, their working interactions. What a musician does in one place will be useful to a writer somewhere else, a scientist makes completely different regimes move, a painter is caused to jump by a percussion: these are not encounters between domains, for each domain is already made up of such encounters in itself. There are only intermezzos, intermezzi, as sources of creation. This is what a conversation is, and not the talk or the preformed debate of specialists amongst themselves, not even an interdisciplinarity which would be ordered in a common project. Oh, of course, the old schools and the new marketing do not exhaust our possibilities; everything that is alive happens elsewhere and is produced elsewhere. There could be a charter for intellectuals, writers, artists, in which they would speak of their refusal to be domesticated by newspapers, radios, TVs, even if this means forming production groups and imposing connections between the creative functions and the dumb functions of those who don't have the means or the right to speak. Above all it's not a question of speaking for the unhappy, of speaking in the name of victims, of the tortured and the oppressed, but of producing a living line, a broken line. The advantage would be – at least in the intellectual world, however small it is – of separating those who want to be 'authors', to form schools or engage in marketing, placing their narcissistic films, their interviews, their broadcasts and their moods (the shame of today), and those who dream of something else – they don't dream, that happens by itself. The two dangers are the intellectual as master or disciple, or else the intellectual as executive, middle or senior executive.

What matters on a path, what matters on a line, is always the middle, not the beginning or the end. We are always in the middle of a path, in the middle of something. The boring thing about questions and answers, about interviews, about conversions, is that usually it's a matter of taking stock: the past and the present, the present and the future. This is why it is even and always possible to say of an author that his first work already contains the whole, or on the contrary that he is ceaselessly renewing himself, transforming himself. In every case it is the theme of the embryo which evolves, sometimes on the basis of a preformation in the seed, sometimes on the basis of successive structurations. But the embryo, evolution, are not good things. Becoming does not happen in that way. In becoming there is no past nor future – not even present, there is no history. In becoming it is, rather, a matter of involuting; it's neither regression nor progression. To become is to become more and more restrained, more and more simple, more and more deserted and for that very reason populated. This is what's difficult to explain: to what extent one should involute. It is obviously the opposite of evolution, but it is also the opposite of regression, returning to a childhood or to a primitive world. To involute is to have an increasingly simple, economical, restrained step. It is also true for clothes: elegance as the opposite of the overdressed where too much is put on, where something more is always added which will spoil everything (English elegance against Italian overdressedness). It is also true of cooking: against evolutive cooking, which always adds something more, against regressive cooking which returns to primary elements, there is involutive cooking, which is perhaps that of the anorexic. Why is there such an elegance in certain anorexics? It is also true of life, even of the most animal kind: if the animals invented their forms and their functions, this was not always by evolving, by developing themselves, nor by regressing as in the case of prematuration, but by losing, by abandoning, by reducing, by simplifying, even if this means creating new elements and new relations of this simplification.[12] Experimentation is involutive, the opposite of the overdose. It is also true of writing; to reach this sobriety, this simplicity which is neither the end nor the beginning of something. To involute is to be 'between', in the middle, adjacent. Beckett's characters are in perpetual in-volution, always in the middle of a path, already *en route*. If one has to hide, if one always has to put on a mask, this is not because of a taste for the secret which would be a little personal secret, nor as a precaution – it is because of a secret of a higher nature, that is, that the path has no beginning or end, that it is in its nature to keep its beginning and end hidden, because it cannot do otherwise. If not it would no longer be a path, it only exists as path in the middle. The dream would be that you are Félix's mask and Félix is yours. Then there would really be a path between the two, that someone else could take in the middle, even if in his turn, etc. That's it, a rhizome, or weed. Embryos, trees, develop according to their genetic preformation or their structural reorganizations. But the weed overflows by virtue of being restrained. It grows between. It is the path itself. The English and the Americans, who are the least 'author-like' of writers, have two particularly sharp directions which connect: that of the road and of the path, that of the grass and of the rhizome. Perhaps this is the reason that they hardly have such a thing as philosophy as a specialized institution and don't have any need for it, because they were able in their novels to make writing an act of thought and life a non-personal power, grass and path in one another, becoming-bison. Henry Miller: 'Grass only exists between the great non-cultivated spaces. It fills in the voids. *It grows between – among the other things.* The flower is beautiful, the cabbage is useful, the poppy makes you crazy. But the grass is overflowing, it is a lesson in morality.'[13] The walk as act, as politics, as experimentation, as life: 'I spread myself out like fog BETWEEN the people that I know the best' says Virginia Woolf in her walk among the taxis.

The middle has nothing to do with an average, it is not a centrism or a form of moderation. On the contrary, it's a matter of absolute speed. Whatever grows from the middle is endowed with such a speed. We must distinguish not relative and absolute movement, but the relative and absolute speed of any movement. The relative is the speed of one movement considered from the point of view of another. But the absolute is the speed of movement between the two, in the middle of the two, which traces a line of flight. Movement does not go from one point to another – rather it happens between two levels as in a difference of potential. A difference of intensity produces a phenomenon, releases or ejects it, sends it into space. Absolute speed can measure a rapid movement, but not a very slow movement or even an immobility, like a movement on the spot. The problem of an absolute speed of thought: there are some strange statements by Epicurus on this theme. Isn't this what Nietzsche does with an aphorism? Thought should be thrown like a stone by a war-machine. Absolute speed is the speed of nomads, even when they move about slowly. Nomads are always in the middle. The steppe always grows from the middle, it is between the great forests and the great empires. The steppe, the grass and the nomads are the same thing. The nomads have neither past nor future, they have only becomings, woman-becoming, animal-becoming, horse-becoming: their extraordinary animalist art. Nomads have no history, they only have geography. Nietzsche: 'They come like destiny, without cause, without reason, without consideration, without pretext.' Kafka: 'It is impossible to understand how they have got as far as the capital; however, they are there and each morning seem to increase their number.' Kleist: 'The Amazons arrive and the Greeks and the Trojans, the two elements of States, each believe that they come as allies but they pass between the two and, along the whole length of their passage, they overthrow both on the line of flight . . .' You and Félix, you produce the hypothesis that the nomads invented the war-machine. Which implies that the States don't have one, and that the power of the state was founded on something else. It was an immensely important task for States to try to appropriate the war-machine by making it into a military institution or an army, in order to turn it against the nomads. But States will always have a lot of difficulty with their armies.

And the war-machine is not primarily a component of the State apparatus. The nomads invented a whole numerical organization which can be found in armies (dozens, hundreds, etc.). This original organization implies relationships with women, plants, animals and metals which are very different from those which are codified in a State. To make thought a nomadic power is not necessarily to move, but it is to shake the model of the state apparatus, the idol or image which weighs down thought, the monster squatting on it. To give thought an absolute speed, a war-machine, a geography and all these becomings or these paths which criss-cross a steppe. Epicurus, Spinoza and Nietzsche as nomad thinkers.

This question of speed is important and also very complex. It doesn't mean the first in the race: you can be late through speed. It doesn't mean changing either: you can be invariable and constant through speed. Speed is to be caught in a becoming – which is not a development or an evolution. One must be like a taxi, queue [*ligne d'attente*], line of flight, traffic jam, bottleneck, green and red lights, slightly paranoid, brushes with the police. To be an abstract and broken line, a zigzag which glides 'between'. The grass and speed. What you mis-named style just now – charm or style – is speed. Children go fast because they know how to glide in between. Fanny imagines the same thing of old age: there is also an old-becoming which defines successful old ages, that is an ageing-quick which is opposed to the ordinary impatience of old people, to their despotism, to their evening-anxiety (cf. the nasty phrase 'life is too short'). Ageing quick, according to Fanny, is not to age precociously, on the contrary, it would be that patience which really allows the grasping of all the speeds which pass. Now, it is exactly the same for writing. Writing ought to produce speed. This doesn't mean writing rapidly. Whether it's Céline, or Paul Morand whom Céline admired ('He has jazzed up the French language'), or Miller: there are astonishing productions of speed. And what Nietzsche did with German – that's what it's like to be a foreigner in one's

own language. It is in writing which is worked over most
slowly that you reach this absolute speed, which is not an
effect but a product. The speed of music, even the most slow.
Is it by chance that music only knows lines and not points? It
is not possible to produce a point in music. It's nothing but
becomings without future or past. Music is an anti-memory.
It is full of becomings: animal-becoming, child-becoming,
molecular-becoming. Steve Reich wants everything to be
perceived in act in music, wants the process to be completely
understood: therefore this music is the slowest, but because it
makes us perceive all the differential speeds. A work of art
must at least mark the seconds. It's like the fixed plane: a way
of making us perceive all that there is in the image. Absolute
speed, which makes us perceive everything at the same time,
can be characteristic of slowness or even of immobility. Immanence. It is exactly the opposite of development, where the
transcendent principle which determines and structures it
never appears directly on its own account, in perceptible
relation with a process, with a becoming. When Fred Astaire
dances the waltz, it is not 1, 2, 3, it is infinitely more detailed.
The tom-tom is not 1, 2. When Blacks dance, they are not
seized by a rhythm demon, they hear and perform all the
notes, all the times, all the tones, all the pitches, all the
intensities, all the intervals. It's never 1, 2, or 1, 2, 3, it's 7, 10,
14 or 28 primary times as in Turkish music. We rediscover
this question of speeds and slownesses – how they are made
up, and above all how they proceed to very special individuations, how they produce individuations without a 'subject'.

A conversation is not made easy if you refrain from taking
stock and don't allow yourself recollections. But there's
another difficulty. You and Félix (Félix is more rapid than
you), you constantly attack dualisms. You say that binary
machines are apparatuses of power to break up becomings:
you are man or woman, white or black, thinker or 'liver',
bourgeois or proletarian? But what are you doing if not pro-

posing other dualisms? Acts of thought without image against the image of thought; rhizome or grass against the trees; the war-machine against the state apparatus; complex multiplicities against unifications and totalizations, the force of forgetting against memory; geography against history; the line against the point, etc. Perhaps it's necessary to·say that language is profoundly wrought by dualisms and dichotomies, divisions by 2, binary calculations: masculine–feminine, singular–plural, nominal syntagm–verbal syntagm.

Linguistics only finds in language what is already there: the arborescent system of hierarchy and command. The I, the YOU, the HE, is very much a part of language. We must speak like everyone else, we must pass through dualisms, 1–2, or even 1–2–3. It must not be said that language deforms a reality which is pre-existing or of another nature. Language is first, it has invented the dualism. But the cult of language, the setting-up of language, linguistics itself, is worse than the old ontology from which it has taken over. We must pass through [*passer par*] dualisms because they are in language, it's not a question of getting rid of them, but we must fight against language, invent stammering, not in order to get back to a prelinguistic pseudo-reality, but to trace a vocal or written line which will make language flow between these dualisms, and which will define a minority usage of language, an inherent variation as Labov says.

In the second place, it is probable that a multiplicity is not defined by the number of its terms. We can always add a 3rd to 2, a 4th to 3, etc., we do not escape dualism in this way, since the elements of any set whatever can be related to a succession of choices which are themselves binary. It is not the elements or the sets which define the multiplicity. What defines it is the AND, as something which has its place between the elements or between the sets. AND, AND, AND —stammering. And even if there are only two terms, there is an AND between the two, which is neither the one nor the other, nor the one which becomes the other, but which constitutes the multiplicity. This is why it is always possible to undo dualisms from the inside, by tracing the line of flight which passes between the two terms or the two sets, the narrow stream which belongs neither to the one nor to the other, but draws both into a non-parallel evolution, into a heterochronous becoming. At least this does not belong to the dialectic. Thus we could proceed like this: each chapter would remain divided in two, there would no longer be any reason to sign each part, since it is between the two anonymous parts that the conversation would take place, and the AND Félix, AND Fanny, AND you, AND all those of whom we speak, AND me, would appear as so many distorted images in running water.

C.P.

2

On the Superiority of Anglo-American Literature

I

To leave, to escape, is to trace a line. The highest aim of literature, according to Lawrence, is 'To leave, to leave, to escape . . . to cross the horizon, enter into another life . . . It is thus that Melville finds himself in the middle of the Pacific. He has really crossed the line of the horizon.' The line of flight is a deterritorialization. The French do not understand this very well. Obviously, they flee like everyone else, but they think that fleeing means making an exit from the world, mysticism or art, or else that it is something rather sloppy because we avoid our commitments and responsibilities. But to flee is not to renounce action: nothing is more active than a flight. It is the opposite of the imaginary. It is also to put to flight – not necessarily others, but to put something to flight, to put a system to flight as one bursts a tube. George Jackson wrote from prison: 'It may be that I am fleeing, but throughout my flight, I am searching for a weapon.' And Lawrence again: 'I tell you, old weapons go rotten: make some new ones and shoot accurately.' To fly is to trace a line, lines, a whole cartography. One only discovers worlds through a long, broken flight. Anglo-American literature constantly shows these ruptures, these characters who create their line of flight, who create through a line of flight. Thomas Hardy, Melville, Stevenson, Virginia Woolf, Thomas Wolfe, Lawrence, Fitzgerald, Miller, Kerouac. In them everything is departure, becoming, passage, leap, daemon, relationship with the outside. They create a new Earth; but perhaps the movement of the earth is deterritorialization itself. American literature operates according to geographical lines: the flight towards the West, the discovery that the true East is in the West, the sense of the frontiers as something to cross, to push back, to go beyond.[1] The becoming is geographical. There is no equivalent in France. The French are too human, too historical, too concerned with the future and the past. They spend their time in in-depth analysis. They do not know how to become, they think in terms of historical past and future. Even with the revolution, they think about a 'future of the revolution' rather than a revolutionary-becoming. They do not know how to trace lines, to follow a channel. They do not know how to pierce or plane down the wall. They are too fond of roots, trees, the survey, the points of arborescence, the properties. Look at structuralism: it is a system of points and positions, which operates by cuts which are supposedly significant instead of proceeding by thrusts and crackings. It warps the lines of flight instead of following them and tracing them and extending them in a social field.

Is it in Michelet, the fine extract in which the kings of France are contrasted with the kings of England: the former with their politics of land, of inheritance, of marriages, of lawsuits, of ruses and cheating, the latter with their movement of deterritorialization, their wanderings and renunciations, their betrayals passing by at breakneck speed? They unleash the flood of capitalism, but the French invent the bourgeois apparatus of power capable of blocking them, of calling them to account.

To flee is not exactly to travel, or even to move. First because there are travels in the style of the French − too historical, cultural and organized − where they are content to transport their own 'egos'. Secondly, because flights can happen on the spot, in motionless travel. Toynbee shows that nomads in the strict, geographical sense are neither migrants nor travellers, but, on the contrary, those who do not move, those who cling on to the steppe, who are immobile with big strides, following a line of flight on the spot, the greatest inventors of new weapons.[2] But history has never begun to understand nomads, who have neither past nor future. Maps are maps of intensities, geography is no less mental and corporeal than physical in movement. When Lawrence takes up cudgels against Melville, he criticizes him for having taken the voyage too seriously. The voyage turns out to be a return to the savage, but such a return is a regression. There is always a way of reterritorializing oneself in the voyage: it is always one's father or mother (or worse) that one finds again on the voyage. 'Going back to the savages made Melville sicker than anything . . . And once he has escaped, immediately he begins to sigh and pine for the "Paradise", Home and Mother being at the other end of a whaling voyage.'[3] Fitzgerald puts it even better: 'This led me to the idea that the ones who had survived had made some sort of clean break. This is a big word and is no parallel to a jail-break when one is probably headed for a new jail or will be forced back to the old one. The famous "escape" or "run away from it all" is an excursion into a trap even if the trap includes the South Seas, which are only for those who want to paint them or sail them. A clean break is something you cannot come back from; that is irretrievable because it makes the past cease to exist.'[4]

But even when a distinction is drawn between the flight and the voyage, the flight still remains an ambiguous operation. What is it which tells us that, on a line of flight, we will not rediscover everything we were fleeing? In fleeing the eternal mother-father, will we not rediscover all the Oedipal structures on the line of flight? In fleeing fascism, we rediscover fascist coagulations on the line of flight. In fleeing everything, how can we avoid reconstituting both our country of origin and our formations of power, our intoxicants, our psychoanalyses and our mummies and daddies? How can one avoid the line of flight's becoming identical with a pure and simple movement of self-destruction; Fitzgerald's alcoholism, Lawrence's disillusion, Virginia Woolf's suicide, Kerouac's

sad end? English and American literature is thoroughly imbued with a sombre process of demolition, which carries off
the writer. A happy death? But it is this that can only be
understood on the line, at the same time as it is being traced:
the dangers which are courted, the patience and precautions
which must go into avoiding them, the corrections which must
constantly be made to extract the line from the quicksands
and the black holes. Prediction is not possible. A true break
may be extended in time, it is something different from an
over-significant cut, it must constantly be protected not
merely against its false imitations, but also against itself, and
against the reterritorializations which lie in wait for it. This is
why it jumps from one writer to another like something which
must be begun again. The English and the Americans do not
have the same way of beginning again as the French. French
beginning again is the *tabula rasa*, the search for a primary
certainty as a point of origin, always the point of anchor. The
other way of beginning again, on the other hand, is to take up
the interrupted line, to join a segment to the broken line, to
make it pass between two rocks in a narrow gorge, or over the
top of the void, where it had stopped. It is never the beginning
or the end which are interesting; the beginning and end are
points. What is interesting is the middle. The English zero is
always in the middle. Bottlenecks are always in the middle.
Being in the middle of a line is the most uncomfortable position. One begins again through the middle. The French think
in terms of trees too much: the tree of knowledge, points of
arborescence, the alpha and omega, the roots and the
pinnacle. Trees are the opposite of grass. Not only does grass
grow in the middle of things, but it grows itself through the
middle. This is the English or American problem. Grass has
its line of flight, and does not take root. We have grass in the
head, not a tree: what thinking signifies is what the brain is, a
'particular nervous system' of grass.[5]

Take as an example the case of Thomas Hardy: his characters are not people or subjects, they are collections of intensive

sensations, each is such a collection, a packet, a bloc of variable sensations. There is a strange respect for the individual, an extraordinary respect: not because he would seize upon himself as a person and be recognized as a person, in the French way, but on the contrary because he saw himself and saw others as so many 'unique chances' – the unique chance from which one combination or another had been drawn. Individuation without a subject. And these packets of sensations in the raw, these collections or combinations, run along the lines of chance, or mischance, where their encounters take place – if need be, their bad encounters which lead to death, to murder. Hardy invokes a sort of Greek destiny for this empiricist experimental world. Individuals, packets of sensations, run over the heath like a line of flight or a line of deterritorialization of the earth.

A flight is a sort of delirium.[6*] To be delirious [*délirer*] is exactly to go off the rails (as in *déconner* – to say absurd things, etc.). There is something demonaical or demonic in a line of flight. Demons are different from gods, because gods have fixed attributes, properties and functions, territories and codes: they have to do with rails, boundaries and surveys. What demons do is jump across intervals, and from one interval to another. 'Which demon has leapt the longest leap?' asks Oedipus. There is always betrayal in a line of flight. Not trickery like that of an orderly man ordering his future, but betrayal like that of a simple man who no longer has any past or future. We betray the fixed powers which try to hold us back, the established powers of the earth. The movement of betrayal has been defined as a double turning-away: man turns his face away from God, who also turns his face away from man. It is in this double turning-away, in the divergence of faces, that the line of flight – that is, the deterritorialization of man – is traced. Betrayal is like theft, it is always double. Oedipus at Colonnus, with his long wanderings, has been taken as the prime example of a double turning-away. But Oedipus is the only Semitic tragedy of the Greeks. God who

turns away from man who turns away from God is the
primary theme of the Old Testament. It is the story of Cain,
Cain's line of flight. It is the story of Jonah: the prophet is
recognizable by the fact that he takes the opposite path to that
which is ordered by God and thereby realizes God's com-
mandment better than if he had obeyed. A traitor, he has
taken misfortune upon himself. The Old Testament is constantly criss-crossed by these lines of flight, the line of separation between the earth and the waters. 'Let the elements stop
kissing, and turn their backs on one another. Let the merman
turn away from his human wife and children . . . Cross the
seas, cross the seas, urges the heart. Leave love and home.'[7]
The 'great discoveries', the great expeditions, do not merely
involve uncertainty as to what will be discovered, the conquest of the unknown, but the invention of a line of flight, and
the power of treason: to be the only traitor, and traitor to all –
Aguirre, Wrath of God. Christopher Columbus, as Jacques
Besse describes him in an extraordinary tale, including the
woman-becoming of Columbus.[8] The creative theft of the
traitor, as against the plagiarisms of the trickster.

The Old Testament is not an epic, or a tragedy, but the first
novel, and it is as such that the English understand it, as the
foundation of the novel. The traitor is the essential character
of the novel, the hero. A traitor to the world of dominant
significations, and to the established order. This is quite
different from the trickster: for the trickster claims to take
possession of fixed properties, or to conquer a territory, or
even to introduce a new order. The trickster has plenty of
future, but no becoming whatsoever. The priest, the
soothsayer, is a trickster, but the experimenter is a traitor.
The statesman or the courtier is a trickster, but the man of
war (not a marshal or a general) is a traitor. The French novel
gives us many tricksters, and our novelists are often tricksters
themselves. They have no special relationship with the Old
Testament. Shakespeare put on the stage many trickster-
kings, who came to the throne by trickery, and who in the last

analysis turn out to be good kings. But when he encounters Richard III he rises to the height of the most novelistic of tragedies. For Richard III does not simply want power, he wants treason. He does not want the conquest of the state, but the assemblage of a war-machine: how can he be the only traitor, and betray all simultaneously? The dialogue with Lady Anne, which critics have judged to be 'improbable and exaggerated', shows the two faces which are turning away, and Anne, already consenting and fascinated, has a presentiment of the tortuous line which Richard is tracing. And nothing reveals treason better than the choice of object. Not because it is a choice of object – a poor notion – but because it is a becoming, it is the demonic element *par excellence*. In his choice of Anne there is a woman-becoming in Richard III. Of what is Captain Ahab in Melville guilty? Of having chosen Moby Dick, the white whale, instead of obeying the law of the group of fishermen, according to which all whales are fit to hunt. In that lies Ahab's demonic element, his treason, his relationship with Leviathan – this choice of object which engages him in a whale-becoming himself. The same theme appears in Kleist's *Penthesilea*: the sin of Penthesilea, to have chosen Achilles while the law of the Amazons ordains that they should not choose the enemy: Penthesilea's demonic element leads her into a dog-becoming. (Kleist appalled the Germans, who did not recognize him as one of them: in his long excursions on horseback, Kleist was one of the authors who, despite the German order, knew how to trace a dazzling line of flight across forests and states. Likewise Lenz or Buchner, all the anti-Goethes.) We must define a special function, which is identical neither with health nor illness: the function of the *Anomalous*. The Anomalous is always at the frontier, on the border of a band or a multiplicity; it is part of the latter, but is already making it pass into another multiplicity, it makes it become, it traces a line-between. This is also the 'outsider':[9*] Moby Dick, or the Thing or Entity of Lovecraft, terror.

It is possible that writing has an intrinsic relationship with lines of flight. To write is to trace lines of flight which are not imaginary, and which one is indeed forced to follow, because in reality writing involves us there, draws us in there. To write is to become, but has nothing to do with becoming a writer. That is to become something else. A writer by profession can judge himself in the light of his past or his future, in the light of his personal future, or of posterity ('I will be understood in two years, in a hundred years,' etc.). The becomings contained in writing when it is not wedded to established order-words, but itself traces lines of flight are quite different. You might say that writing by itself, when it is not official, necessarily comes into contact with 'minorities' who do not necessarily write on their own account, about whom no one writes either, in the sense that they would be taken as object, but, on the contrary, in which one is caught up willy-nilly, from the fact that one is writing. A minority never exists ready-made, it is only formed on lines of flight, which are also its way of advancing and attacking. There is a woman-becoming in writing. *Madame Bovary, c'est moi* is the sentence of a hysterical trickster. Even women do not always succeed when they force themselves to write like women, as a function of a future of woman. Woman is not necessarily the writer, but the minority-becoming of her writing, whether it be man or woman. Virginia Woolf forbade herself 'to speak like a woman': she harnessed the woman-becoming of writing all the more for this. Lawrence and Miller are considered to be great sexists: writing, however, drew them into an irresistible woman-becoming. It is only through this becoming, where women have to make as much effort as men, that England has produced so many women novelists. There are the Negro-becomings in writing, Indian-becomings which do not consist in speaking American Indian or 'pidgin French'. There are animal-becomings in writing which do not consist in imitating the animal, in 'playing' the animal, any more than Mozart's music imitates birds, although it is imbued with a bird-becoming. Captain Ahab has a whale-becoming which is not one of imitation. Lawrence has the tortoise-becoming, in his admirable poems. There are animal-becomings in literature which do not consist in talking of one's dog or cat. It is rather an encounter between two reigns, a short-circuit, the picking-up of a code where each is deterritorialized. In writing one always gives writing to those who do not have it, but the latter give writing a becoming without which it would not exist, without which it would be pure redundancy in the service of the powers that be. That the writer is minoritarian does not mean that there are fewer people who write than read; this would no longer even be true today: it means that writing always encounters a minority which does not write, and it does not undertake to write for this minority, in its place or at its bidding, but there is an encounter in which each pushes the other, draws it on to its line of flight in a combined deterritorialization. Writing always combines with something else, which is its own becoming. There is no assemblage which functions on a single flux. This is not a matter of imitation, but of conjunction. The writer is imbued to the core with a non-writer-becoming. Hofmannsthal (who then adopts an English pseudonym) can no longer write when he sees the agony of a mob of rats, because he senses that it is in him that the animal's soul bares its teeth. A fine English film, *Willard*, showed the irresistible rat-becoming of the hero, who clutched at humanity at every chance but nevertheless found himself drawn into this fatal coupling. That there are so many writers' silences and suicides must be explained by these nuptials against nature, these collaborations against nature. What other reason is there for writing than to be traitor to one's own reign, traitor to one's sex, to one's class, to one's majority? And to be traitor to writing.

Many people dream of being traitors. They believe in it, they believe that they are. But they are just petty tricksters. Take the pathetic case of Maurice Sachs, in French literature. What trickster has not said to himself: 'Oh, at last I am a real traitor.' But what traitor does not say to himself at the day's end: 'After all, I was nothing but a trickster.' For it is difficult to be a traitor; it is to create. One has to lose one's identity, one's face, in it. One has to disappear, to become unknown. The aim, the finality of writing? Still way beyond a woman-becoming, a Negro-becoming, an animal-becoming, etc., beyond a minority-becoming, there is the final enterprise of the becoming-imperceptible. Oh no, a writer cannot wish to be 'known', recognized. The imperceptible, common characteristic of the greatest speed and the greatest slowness. Writing has no other end than to lose one's face, to jump over or pierce through the wall, to plane down the wall very patiently. This is what Fitzgerald called a true break: the line of flight, not the voyage into the South Seas, the acquisition of a clandestinity (even if one has to become animal, to become Negro or woman). To be unknown at last, as are very few people, is to betray. It is very difficult not to be known at all, even by one's landlady or in one's neighbourhood, the nameless singer, the ritornello. At the end of *Tender is the Night*, the hero literally dissipates himself geographically. That text of Fitzgerald's which is so fine, *The Crack-Up*, says: 'I felt like the men whom I used to see in the suburban trains of Great Neck fifteen years before . . .' There is a whole social system which might be called the white wall/black hole system. We are always pinned against the wall of dominant significations, we are always sunk in the hole of our subjectivity, the black hole of our Ego which is more dear to us than anything. A wall on which are inscribed all the objective determinations which fix us, put us into a grille, identify us and make us recognized, a hole where we deposit − together with our consciousness − our feelings, our passions, our little secrets which are all too well known, our desire to make them known. Even if the face is a product of this system, it is a social production: a broad face with white cheeks, with the black hole of the eyes. Our societies need to produce the face. Christ invented the face. Miller's problem (like Lawrence's): how to unmake the face, by liberating in ourselves the questing heads which trace the lines of becoming? How to get past the wall while avoiding bouncing back on it, behind, or being crushed? How to get out of the black hole instead of whirling round in its depths, which particles to get out of the black hole? How to shatter even our love in order to become finally capable of loving? How to become imperceptible?

> I no longer look into the eyes of the woman I hold in my arms, but I swim through, head and arms and legs, and I see that behind the sockets of the eyes there is a region unexplored, a world of futurity, and here there is no logic whatever . . . this selfless eye neither reveals nor illuminates. It travels along the line of the horizon, a ceaseless, uninformed voyager . . . I have broken the wall created by birth and the line of voyage is round and un-broken . . . My whole body must become a constant beam of light, moving with an ever greater rapidity . . . Therefore I close my ears, my eyes, my mouth. Before I shall become quite man again, I shall probably exist as a park . . .[10]

There we no longer have any secrets, we no longer have anything to hide. It is we who have become a secret, it is we who are hidden, even though we do all openly, in broad daylight. This is the opposite of the romanticism of the 'damned'.[11*] We have painted ourselves in the colours of the world. Lawrence condemned the craze for 'the dirty little secret', which he saw as running through all French literature. The characters and the authors always have a little secret, on which the craze for interpretation feeds. Something must always remind us of something else, make us think of some-thing else. We remember Oedipus' dirty little secret, not the Oedipus of Colonnus, on his line of flight, who has become imperceptible, identical to the great living secret. The great secret is when you no longer have anything to hide, and thus when no one can grasp you. A secret everywhere, no more to be said. Since the 'signifier' has been invented, things have not fallen into place. Instead of language being interpreted by us, it has set about interpreting us, and interpreting itself. Significance and interpretosis are the two diseases of the earth, the pair of despot and priest. The signifier is always the little secret which has never stopped hanging around mummy and daddy. We blackmail ourselves, we make ourselves out to be mysterious, discreet, we move with the air of saying 'See how I am weighed down by a secret.' The thorn in the flesh. The little secret is generally reducible to a sad narcissistic and pious masturbation: the phantasm! 'Transgression', a concept too good for seminarists under the law of a Pope or a priest, the tricksters. Georges Bataille is a very French author. He made the little secret the essence of literature, with a mother within, a priest beneath, an eye above. It is impossible to overemphasize the harm that the phantasm has done to writing (it has even invaded the cinema) in sustaining the signifier, and the interpretation of one by the other, of one with the other. 'The world of phantasms is a world of the past', a theatre of resentment and guilt. You see many people today one after another proclaiming 'Long live castration, for it is the home, the Origin and the End of desire!' What is in the middle is forgotten. New races of priests are always being invented for the dirty little secret, which has no other object than to get itself recognized, to put us back into a very black hole, to bounce us off the very white wall.

Your secret can always be seen on your face and in your eyes. Lose your face. Become capable of loving without remembering, without phantasm and without interpretation, without taking stock. Let there just be fluxes, which sometimes dry up, freeze or overflow, which sometimes combine or diverge. A man and a woman are fluxes. All the becomings which there are in making love, all the sexes, the n sexes in a single one, or in two, which have nothing to do with castration. On lines of flight there can no longer be but one thing, life-experimentation. One never knows in advance, since one no longer has either future or past. 'See me as I am':

all that stuff is over. There is no longer a phantasm, but only programmes of life, always modified in the process of coming into being, betrayed in the process of being hollowed out, like banks which are disposed or canals which are arranged in order that a flux may flow. There are now only voyages of exploration in which one always finds in the West that which one had thought to be in the East, organs reversed. Every line in which someone gets carried away is a line of restraint in comparison with the laborious, precise, controlled trash of French writers. No longer is there the infinite account of interpretations which are always slightly disgusting, but finished processes of experimentation, protocols of experience. Kleist and Kafka spent their time making programmes for life. Programmes are not manifestos – still less are they phantasms, *but means of providing reference points for an experiment which exceeds our capacities to foresee* (likewise, what is called programme music). The strength of Castaneda's books, in his programmed experiment with drugs, is that each time the interpretations are dismantled and the famous signifier is eliminated. No, the dog I saw and ran along with under the effect of the drug was not my whore of a mother . . . This is a procedure of animal-becoming which does not try to say anything other than what he becomes, and makes me become with him. Other becomings will link up here, molecular-becomings in which the air, sound, water are grasped in their particles at the same time as their flux combines with mine. A whole world of micro-perceptions which lead us to the imperceptible. Experiment, never interpret. Make programmes, never make phantasms. Henry James, who is one of those to have penetrated most deeply the woman-becoming of writing, invents a post-office girl, a heroine caught in a telegraphic flux, which at the start she dominates, thanks to her 'prodigious art of interpretation' (evaluating the senders, the anonymous or coded telegrams). But from fragment to fragment is constructed a living experiment in which interpretation begins to crumble, in which there is no longer perception or knowledge, secret or divination. 'She had ended up knowing so much about it that she could no longer interpret, there were no longer obscurities which made her see clearly . . . *all that was left was a garish light.*' English or American literature is a process of experimentation. They have killed interpretation.

The great and only error lines in thinking that a line of flight consists in fleeing from life; the flight into the imaginary, or into art. On the contrary, to flee is to produce the real, to create life, to find a weapon. Generally it is in the same false movement that life is reduced to something personal and that the work is supposed to find its end in itself, whether as total work, or work in the process of being created, which always refers back to a writing of writing. This is why French literature abounds in manifestos, in ideologies, in theories of writing, at the same time as in personal conflicts, in perfecting of perfectings, in neurotic toadying, in narcissistic tribunals. Writers have their own filthy hovel in life, at the same time as having their land, their motherland, which is all the more spiritual in the work to be created. They are happy to stink personally, since what they write will be all the more sublime and significant. French literature if often the most shameless eulogy of neurosis. The work will be all the more significant for referring to the sly wink and life's little secret, and vice versa. You should hear qualified critics talking of Kleist's failures, Lawrence's impotence, Kafka's childishness, Carroll's little girls. It is unworthy. It is always done with the best intentions: the work will appear all the greater the more pitiful the life is made to seem. There is thus no risk of seeing the power of life which runs through a work. All has been crushed in advance. It is the same resentment, the same taste for castration, which animates the great Signifier as proposed finality of the work, and the little imaginary Signified, the phantasm as suggested expedient of life. Lawrence criticized French literature for being incurably intellectual, ideological and idealist, essentially critical, critical of life rather than creative of life. French nationalism in letters: a terrible mania for judging and being judged runs through that literature: there are too many hysterics among these writers and their characters. Hating, wanting to be loved, but a huge incapacity to love and admire. In reality *writing does not have its end in itself, precisely because life is not something personal.* Or rather, the aim of writing is to carry life to the state of a non-personal power. In doing this it renounces claim to any territory, any end which would reside in itself. Why does one write? Because it is not a case of writing. It may be that the writer has delicate health, a weak constitution. He is none the less the opposite of the neurotic: a sort of great Alive (in the manner of Spinoza, Nietzsche or Lawrence) in so far as he is only too weak for the life which runs in him or for the affects which pass in him. To write has no other function: to be a flux which combines with other fluxes – all the minority-becomings of the world. A flux is something intensive, instantaneous and mutant – between a creation and a destruction. It is only when a flux is de-territorialized that it succeeds in making its conjunction with other fluxes, which deterritorialize it in their turn, and vice versa. In an animal-becoming a man and an animal combine, neither of which resembles the other, neither of which imitates the other, each deterritorializing the other, pushing the line further. A system of relay and mutations through the middle. The line of flight is creative of these becomings. Lines of flight have no territory. Writing carries out the conjunction, the transmutation of fluxes, through which life escapes from the resentment of persons, societies and reigns. Kerouac's phrases are as sober as a Japanese drawing, a pure line traced by an unsupported hand, which passes across ages and reigns. It would take a true alcoholic to attain that degree of sobriety. Or the heath-phrase, the heath-line of Thomas Hardy: it is not that the heath is the subject or the content of the novel, but that a flux of modern writing combines with a flux of immemorial heath. A heath-becoming; or else Miller's grass-becoming, what he calls his China-becoming. Virginia

Woolf and her gift of pasing from one reign to another, from one element to another; did it need Virginia Woolf's anorexia? One only writes through love, all writing is a love-letter: the literature-Real. One should only die through love, and not a tragic death. One should only write through this death, or stop writing through this love, or continue to write, both at once. We know no book of love more important, more insinuating than Kerouac's *The Underground Ones*. He does not ask 'What is writing?', because he has all its necessity, the impossibility of another choice which indeed makes writing, on the condition that for him writing is already another becoming, or comes from another becoming. Writing, the means to a more than personal life, instead of life being a poor secret for a writing which has no end other than itself. Oh, the poverty of the imaginary and the symbolic, the real always being put off until tomorrow.

II

The minimum real unit is not the word, the idea, the concept or the signifier, but the *assemblage*. It is always an assemblage which produces utterances. Utterances do not have as their cause a subject which would act as a subject of enunciation, any more than they are related to subjects as subjects of utterance. The utterance is the product of an assemblage – which is always collective, which brings into play within us and outside us populations, multiplicities, territories, becomings, affects, events. The proper name does not designate a subject, but something which happens, at least between two terms which are not subjects, but agents, elements. Proper names are not names of persons, but of peoples and tribes, flora and fauna, military operations or typhoons, collectives, limited companies and production studios. The author is a subject of enunciation but the writer – who is not an author – is not. The writer invents assemblages starting from assemblages which have invented him, he makes one multiplicity pass into another. The difficult part is making all the elements of a non-homogeneous set converge, making them function together. Structures are linked to conditions of homogeneity, but assemblages are not. The assemblage is co-functioning, it is 'sympathy', symbiosis. With deepest sympathy. Sympathy is not a vague feeling of respect or of spiritual participation: on the contrary, it is the exertion or the penetration of bodies, hatred or love, for hatred is also a compound, it is a body, it is no good except when it is compounded with what it hates. Sympathy is bodies who love or hate each other, each time with populations in play, in these bodies or on these bodies. Bodies may be physical, biological, psychic, social, verbal: they are always bodies or corpora. The author, as subject of enunciation, is first of all a spirit: sometimes he identifies with his characters or makes us identify with them, or with the idea which they represent; sometimes, on the other hand, he introduces a distance which allows him and us to observe, to criticize, to prolong. But this is no good. The author creates a world, but there is no world which awaits us to be created. Neither identification nor distance, neither proximity nor remoteness, for, in all these cases, one is led to speak for, in the place of . . . One must, on the contrary, speak *with*, write *with*. With the world, with a part of the world, with people. Not a talk at all, but a conspiracy, a collision of love or hatred. There is no judgement in sympathy, but agreements of convenience between bodies of all kinds. 'All the subtle sympathies of the soul without number, from the bitterest hatred to the most passionate love.'[12] This is assembling, being in the middle, on the line of encounter between an internal world and the external world. Being in the middle: 'The most important thing . . . is to make . . . [himself] perfectly useless, to be absorbed in the common stream, to become a fish again and not a freak of nature. The only benefit, I reflected, which the act of writing could offer me was to remove the differences which separated me from my fellow man.'[13]

It must be said that it is the world itself which lays the two traps of distance and identification for us. There are many neurotics and lunatics in the world who do not let go of us until they have managed to reduce us to their state, pass us their poison, hysterics, narcissists, their contagion is insidious. There are many doctors and scholars who offer us a sanitized scientific observation, who are also true lunatics, paranoiacs. One must resist both of the traps, the one which offers us the mirror of contamination and identifications, and the one which points out to us the observation of the understanding. We can only assemble among assemblages. We only have sympathy to struggle and to write, Lawrence used to say. But sympathy is something to be reckoned with, it is a bodily struggle, hating what threatens and infects life, loving where it proliferates (no posterity or lineage, but a proliferation . . .). No, says Lawrence, you are not the little Eskimo going by, yellow and greasy, you do not need to mistake yourself for him. But you may perhaps put yourself in his shoes, you have something to assemble with him, an Eskimo-becoming which does not consist in playing the Eskimo, in imitating or identifying yourself with him or taking the Eskimo upon yourself, but in assembling something between you and him, for you can only become Eskimo if the Eskimo himself becomes something else. The same goes for lunatics, drug addicts, alcoholics. I hear the objection: with your puny sympathy you make use of lunatics, you sing the praises of madness, then you drop them, you only go so far . . . This is not true. We are trying to extract from love all possession, all identification to become capable of loving. We are trying to extract from madness the life which it contains, while hating the lunatics who constantly kill life, turn it against itself. We are trying to extract from alcohol the life which it contains, without drinking: the great scene of drunkenness on pure water in Henry Miller. Becoming is loving without alcohol, drugs and madness, becoming-sober for a life which is richer and richer. This is sympathy, assembling. Making one's bed, the opposite of making a career, being neither simulator of identifications nor the frigid doctor of distances. You will get into your bed as you made it, no one will come to tuck you in. Too many people want to be tucked in by a huge identifying mother, or by the social medical officer of distances. Yes, lunatics, madmen, neurotics, alcoholics and drug addicts, the infectious ones, let them get out of it as best they can: our very sympathy is that it should be none of our business. Each one of us has to make his own way. But being capable of it is sometimes difficult.

A rule of these conversations: the longer a paragraph, the more it is suited to being read very quickly. And the repetitions ought to function as accelerations. Certain examples will recur constantly: WASP and ORCHID, or HORSE and STIRRUP. One might put forward many others, but returning to the same example should lead to acceleration, even at the risk of wearying the reader. A ritornello? All music, all writing takes that course. It is the conversation itself which will be a ritornello.

On Empiricism

Why write, why have written about empiricism, and about Hume in particular? Because empiricism is like the English novel. It is a case of philosophizing as a novelist, of being a novelist in philosophy. Empiricism is often defined as a doctrine according to which the intelligible 'comes' from the sensible, everything in the understanding comes from the senses. But that is the standpoint of the history of philosophy: they have the gift of stifling all life in seeking and in positing an abstract first principle. Whenever one believes in a great first principle, one can no longer produce anything but huge sterile dualisms. Philosophers willingly surrender themselves to this and centre their discussions on what should be the first principle (Being, the Ego, the Sensible? . . .). But it is not really worth invoking the concrete richness of the sensible if it is only to make it into an abstract principle. In fact the first principle is always a mask, a simple image. That does not exist, things do not start to move and come alive until the level of the second, third, fourth principle, and these are no longer even principles. Things do not begin to live except in the middle. In this respect what is it that the empiricists found, not in their heads, but in the world, which is like a vital discovery, a certainty of life which, if one really adheres to it, changes one's way of life? It is not the question 'Does the intelligible come from the sensible?' but a quite different question, that of relations. *Relations are external to their terms.* 'Peter is smaller than Paul', 'The glass is on the table': relation is neither internal to one of the terms which would consequently be subject, nor to two together. Moreover, a relation may change without the terms changing. One may object that the glass is perhaps altered when it is moved off the table, but that is not true. The ideas of the glass and the table, which are the true terms of the relations, are not altered. Relations are in the middle, and exist as such. This exteriority of relations is not a principle, it is a vital protest against principles. Indeed if one sees in it something which runs through life, but which is repugnant to thought, then thought must be forced to think it, one must make relations the hallucination point of thought, an experimentation which does violence to thought. Empiricists are not theoreticians, they are experimenters: they never interpret, they have no principles. If one takes this exteriority of relations as a conducting wire or as a line, one sees a very strange world unfold, fragment by fragment: a Harlequin's jacket or patchwork, made up of solid parts and voids, blocs and ruptures, attractions and divisions, nuances and bluntnesses, conjunctions and separations, alternations and interweavings, additions which never reach a total and subtractions whose remainder is never fixed. One can see clearly how the pseudo-first principle of empiricism derives from this, but as a negative limit, always being pushed back, a mask put on at the start: in effect if relations are external and irreducible to their terms, then the difference cannot be between the sensible

from judgements of existence and attribution. For nothing as yet prevents relations as they are detected in conjunctions (NOW, THUS, etc.) from remaining subordinate to the verb to be. The whole of grammar, the whole of the syllogism, is a way of maintaining the subordination of conjunctions to the verb to be, of making them gravitate around the verb to be. One must go further: one must make the encounter with relations penetrate and corrupt everything, undermine being, make it topple over. Substitute the AND for IS. A *and* B. The AND is not even a specific relation or conjunction, it is that which subtends all relations, the path of all relations, which makes relations shoot outside their terms and outside the set of their terms, and outside everything which could be determined as Being, One, or Whole. The AND as extra-being, inter-being. Relations might still establish themselves between their terms, or between two sets, from one to the other, but the AND gives relations another direction, and puts to flight terms and sets, the former and the latter on the line of flight which it actively creates. Thinking *with* AND, instead of thinking IS, instead of thinking *for* IS: empiricism has never had another secret. Try it, it is a quite extraordinary thought, and yet it is life. The empiricists think in this way, that is all there is to it. And it is not the thought of an aesthete, as when one says 'one more', 'one more woman'. And it is not a dialectical thought, as when one says 'one gives two, which will give three'. The multiple is no longer an adjective which is still subordinate to the One which divides or the Being which encompasses it. It has become noun, a multiplicity which constantly inhabits each thing. A multiplicity is never in terms, however many there are, nor in their set or totality. A multiplicity is only in the AND, which does not have the same nature as the elements, the sets or even their relations. While it may come about between just two, it nevertheless sends dualism off course. The AND has a fundamental sobriety, a poverty, an ascesis. Apart from Sartre, who remained caught none the less in the trap of the verb to be, the most important philosopher in France was Jean Wahl. He not only introduced us to an encounter with English and American thought, but had the ability to make us think, in French, things which were very new; he on his own account took this art of the AND, this stammering of language in itself, this minoritarian use of language, the furthest.

Is it really surprising that this comes to us from English or American? It is a hegemonic, imperialistic language. But for this reason it is all the more vulnerable to the subterranean workings of languages and dialects which undermine it from all sides and impose on it a play of vast corruptions and variations. Those who campaign for a pure French, uncontaminated by English, are in our view posing a false problem which only has any validity in the discussions of intellectuals. The American language bases its despotic official pretensions, its majoritarian claim to hegemony, only on its extraordinary capacity for being twisted and shattered and for secretly putting itself in the service of minorities who work it from inside, involuntarily, unofficially, nibbling away at that hegemony as it extends itself: the reverse of power. English has always been worked upon by all these minority languages, Gaelic-English, Irish-English, etc., which are all so many war-machines against the English: Synge's AND which takes upon itself all conjunctions, all relations, and 'the way',[14]* the highway, to mark the line of language which is unfolding.[15] American is worked upon by a Black English, and also a Yellow English, a Red English, a broken English, each of which is like a language shot with a spray-gun of colours: the very different use of the verb to be, the different use of conjunctions, the continuous line of the AND . . . and if slaves need to have some knowledge of standard English, it is only in order to flee, and to put language itself to flight.[16] Oh no, it is not a question of imitating patois or restoring dialects like the peasant novelists, who are generally guardians of the established order. It is a case of making language shift, with words which are increasingly restrained and a syntax which is increasingly subtle. It is not a question of speaking a language as if one was a foreigner, it is a question of being a foreigner in one's own language, in the sense that American is indeed the Blacks' language. Anglo-American has a bent for that. One might contrast the way in which English and German form the composite words in which both languages are equally rich. But German is dogged by the primacy of being, the nostalgia for being, and makes all the conjunctions which it uses to create a composite word tend towards it: the cult of the *Grund*, of the tree and roots, of the Inside. English, on the other hand, creates composite words whose only link is an implied AND, relationship with the Outside, cult of the road which never plunges down, which has no foundations, which shoots on the surface, rhizome. Blue-eyed boy:[17*] a boy, some blue, and eyes – an assemblage. AND . . . AND . . . AND, stammering. Empiricism is nothing other than this. It is each major language, more or less gifted, which must be broken, each in its own way, to introduce this creative AND which will make language shoot along, and will make us this stranger in our language, in so far as it is our own. Finding the means proper to French, with its strength of its own minorities, of its own becoming-minor (it is a pity in this respect that many writers suppress punctuation, which in French is equivalent to AND). That is what empiricism is, syntax and experimentation, syntactics and pragmatics, a matter of speed.

On Spinoza

Why write about Spinoza? Here again, let us take him by the middle and not by the first principle (a single substance for all the attributes). The soul AND the body; no one has ever had such an original feeling for the conjunction 'and'. Each individual, body and soul, possesses an infinity of parts which belong to him in a more or less complex relationship. Each individual is also himself composed of individuals of a lower order and enters into the composition of individuals of a higher order. All individuals are in Nature as though on a plane of consistence whose whole figure they form, a plane which is variable at each moment. They affect each other in so far as the relationship which constitutes each one forms a degree of power, a capacity to be affected. Everything is simply an encounter in the universe, a good or a bad encounter. Adam eats the apple, the forbidden fruit. This is a phenomenon of the indigestion, intoxication, poisoning type: this rotten apple decomposes Adam's relationship. Adam has a bad encounter. Whence the force of Spinoza's question: '*What can a body do?*', of what affects is it capable? Affects are becomings: sometimes they weaken us in so far as they diminish our power to act and decompose our relationships (sadness), sometimes they make us stronger in so far as they increase our power and make us enter into a more vast or superior individual (joy). Spinoza never ceases to be amazed by the body. He is not amazed at having a body, but by what the body can do. Bodies are not defined by their genus or species, by their organs and functions, but by what they can do, by the affects of which they are capable – in passion as well as in action. You have not defined an animal until you have listed its affects. In this sense there is a greater difference between a race horse and a work horse than between a work horse and an ox. A distant successor of Spinoza would say: look at the tick, admire that creature; it is defined by three affects, which are all it is capable of as a result of the relationships of which it is composed, nothing but a tri-polar world! Light affects it and it climbs on to the end of a branch. The smell of a mammal affects it and it drops down on to it. The hairs get in its way and it looks for a hairless place to burrow under the skin and drink the warm blood. Blind and deaf, the tick has only three affects in the vast forest, and for the rest of the time may sleep for years awaiting the encounter. What power, nevertheless! Finally, one always has the organs and functions corresponding to the affects of which one is capable. Let us begin with the simple animals who only have a few affects, and who are neither in our world, nor in another, but *with* an associated world that they have learnt how to trim, cut up, sew back together: the spider and his web, the louse and the scalp, the tick and a small patch of mammal skin: these and not the owl of Minerva are the true philosophical beasts. That which triggers off an affect, that which effectuates a power to be affected, is called a signal: the web stirs, the scalp creases, a little skin is bared. Nothing but a few signs like stars in an immense black night. Spider-becoming, flea-becoming, tick-becoming, an unknown, resilient, obscure, stubborn life.

When Spinoza says 'The surprising thing is the body . . . we do not yet know what a body is capable of . . .', he does not want to make the body a model, and the soul simply dependent on the body. He has a subtler task. He wants to demolish the pseudo-superiority of the soul over the body. There is the soul and the body and both express one and the same thing: an attribute of the body is also an expressed of the soul (for example, speed). Just as you do not know what a body is capable of, just as there are many things in the body that you do not know, so there are in the soul many things which go beyond your consciousness. This is the question: what is a body capable of? what affects are you capable of? Experiment, but you need a lot of prudence to experiment. We live in a world which is generally disagreeable, where not only people but the established powers have a stake in transmitting sad affects to us. Sadness, sad affects, are all those which reduce our power to act. The established powers need our sadness to make us slaves. The tyrant, the priest, the captors of souls need to persuade us that life is hard and a burden. The powers that be need to repress us no less than to make us anxious or, as Virilio says, to administer and organize our intimate little fears. The long, universal moan about life: the lack-to-be[18]* which is life . . . In vain someone says, 'Let's dance'; we are not really very happy. In vain someone says, 'What misfortune death is'; for one would need to have lived to have something to lose. Those who are sick, in soul as in body, will not let go of us, the vampires, until they have transmitted to us their neurosis and their anxiety, their beloved castration, the resentment against life, filthy contagion. It is all a matter of blood. It is not easy to be a free man, to flee the plague, organize encounters, increase the power to act, to be moved by joy, to multiply the affects which express or encompass a maximum of affirmation. To make the body a power which is not reducible to the organism, to make thought a power which is not reducible to consciousness. Spinoza's famous first principle (a single substance for all attributes) depends on this assemblage and not vice versa. There is a Spinoza-assemblage: soul and body, relationships and encounters, power to be affected, affects which realize this power, sadness and joy which qualify these affects. Here philosophy becomes the art of a functioning, of an assemblage. Spinoza, the man of encounters and becoming, the philosopher with the tick, Spinoza the imperceptible, always in the middle, always in flight although he does not shift much, a flight from the Jewish community, a flight from the Powers, a flight from the sick and the malignant. He may be ill, he may himself die; he knows that death is neither the goal nor the end, but that, on the contrary, it is a case of passing his life to someone else. What Lawrence says about Whitman's continuous life is well suited to Spinoza: the Soul and the Body, the soul is neither above nor inside, it is 'with', it is on the road, exposed to all contacts, encounters, in the company of those who follow the same way, 'feel with them, seize the vibration of their soul and their body as they pass', the opposite of a morality of salvation, teaching the soul to live its life, not to save it.

On the Stoics

Why write about them? A darker and more agitated world has never been set out: bodies . . . but qualities are also bodies, breaths and souls are bodies, actions and passions themselves are bodies. Everything is a compound of bodies – bodies interpenetrate, force each other, poison each other, insinuate themselves into each other, withdraw, reinforce or destroy each other, as fire penetrates iron and makes it red, as the carnivore devours its prey, as the lover enters the beloved. 'There is flesh in bread, and bread in plants; these bodies and many others enter into all bodies, by hidden channels, and evaporate together . . .' Thyestes' terrible feast, incest and devouring, sicknesses which are nurtured in our thighs, so many bodies which grow in our own. Who is to say which compound is good or bad, since all is good from the viewpoint of the two parties which encounter one another and interpenetrate. Which love is not that of brother and sister, which feast is not cannibalistic? But see how, from all these bodily struggles, there arises a sort of incorporeal vapour, which no longer consists in qualities, in actions or in passions, in causes acting upon one another, but in results of these actions and passions, in effects which result from all these causes together. They are pure, impassive, incorporeal events, on the surface of things, pure infinitives of which it cannot even be said that they ARE, participating rather in an extra-being which surrounds that which is: 'to redden', 'to turn green', 'to cut', 'to die', 'to love' . . . Such an event, such a verb in the infinitive is also the expressed of a proposition or the attribute of a state of things. The Stoics' strength lay in making a line of separation pass – no longer between the sensible and the intelligible, or between the soul and the body, but where no one had seen it before – between physical depth and metaphysical surface. Between things and events. Between states of things and compounds, causes, souls and bodies, actions and passions, qualities and substances on the one hand, and, on the other, events or impassive, unqualifiable, incorporeal Effects, infinitives which result from these amalgams, which are attributed to these states of things, which are expressed in propositions. A new way of getting rid of the IS: the attribute is no longer a quality related to the subject by the indicative 'is', it is any verb whatever in the infinitive which emerges from a state of things and skims over it. Verbs in the infinitive are limitless becomings. The verb to be has the characteristic – like an original taint – of referring to an I, at least to a possible one, which overcodes it and puts it in the first person of the indicative. But infinitive-becomings have no subject: they refer only to an 'it' of the event (it is raining) and are themselves attributed to states of things which are compounds or collectives, assemblages, even at the peak of their singularity. HE – TO WALK – TOWARDS, THE NOMADS – TO ARRIVE, THE – YOUNG – SOLDIER – TO FLEE, THE SCHIZOPHRENIC STUDENT – OF – LANGUAGES – TO STOP – EARS, WASP – TO ENCOUNTER – ORCHID. The telegram is a speed of event, not an economy of means. True propositions are classified advertisements. They are also the elementary units of novels or of events. True novels operate with indefinites which are not indeterminate, infinitives which are not undifferentiated, proper names which are not persons: 'the young soldier' who leaps up and flees and sees himself leap up and flee, in Stephen Crane's book, 'the young student of languages' in Wolfson . . .

There is a strict complementarity between the two; between physical things in the depths and metaphysical events on the surface. How could an event not be effected in bodies, since it depends on a state and on a compound of bodies as its causes, since it is produced by bodies, the breaths and qualities which are interpenetrating here and now? But how, moreover, could the event be exhausted by its effectuation, since, as effect, it differs in nature from its cause, since it acts itself as a quasi-cause which skims over bodies, which traverses and traces a surface, object of a counter-effectuation or of an eternal truth? The event is always produced by bodies which collide, lacerate each other or interpenetrate, the flesh and the sword. But this effect itself is not of the order of bodies, an impassive, incorporeal, impenetrable battle, which towers over its own accomplishment and dominates its effectuation. The question

'Where is the battle?' has constantly been asked. Where is the event, in what does an event consist: each asks this question spontaneously, 'Where is the storming of the Bastille?' Any event is a fog of a million droplets. If the infinitives 'to die', 'to love', 'to move', 'to smile', etc., are events, it is because there is a part of them which their accomplishment is not enough to realize, a becoming in itself which constantly both awaits us and precedes us, like a third person of the infinitive, a fourth person singular. Yes, dying is engendered in our bodies, comes about in our bodies, but it comes from the Outside, singularly incorporeal, falling upon us like the battle which skims over the combatants, like the bird which hovers above the battle. Love is in the depth of bodies, but also on that incorporeal surface which engenders it. So that, agents or patients, when we act or undergo, we must always be worthy of what happens to us. Stoic morality is undoubtedly this: not being inferior to the event, becoming the child of one's own events. The wound is something that I receive in my body, in a particular place, at a particular moment, but there is also an eternal truth of the wound as impassive, incorporeal event. 'My wound existed before me, I was born to embody it!'[19] *Amor fati*, to want the event, has never been to resign oneself, still less to play the clown or the mountebank, but to extract from our actions and passions that surface refulgence, to *counter-effectuate* the event, to accompany that effect without body, that part which goes beyond the accomplishment, the immaculate part. A love of life which can say yes to death. This is the genuinely Stoic transition. Or Lewis Carroll's transition: he is fascinated by the little girl whose body is worked on by so many things in the depths. but over whom skim so many events without substance. We live between two dangers: the eternal groaning of our body, which is always running up against a sharply pointed body which lacerates it, an oversized body which penetrates and stifles it, an indigestible body which poisons it, a piece of furniture which bumps against it, a germ which gives it a pimple: but also the

structural at all. An axiomatics was the extraction of a structure which made the variable elements to which it was applied homogeneous or homologous. This was a recoding operation, the reintroduction of order into the sciences, for science has never ceased to be delirious [*délirer*], to make completely decoded fluxes of knowledge and objects pass along lines of flight, continually going further afield. There is thus a whole politics which demands that the lines should be blocked, that an order should be established. Think, for example, about the role which Louis de Broglie had in physics, in preventing indeterminism from going too far, in calming the madness of particles: a restoration of order. Today it seems rather that the delirium of science is having a revival. It is not just the race to find undiscoverable particles. Science is becoming increasingly event-centred [*événementielle*] instead of structural. It follows lines and circuits, it takes leaps, rather than constructing axiomatics. A sign of this is the disappearance of schemas of arborescence, to give way to rhizomatic movements. Scientists are more and more concerned with singular events, of an incorporal nature, which are effected in bodies, in states of bodies, in completely heterogeneous assemblages (whence the call for interdisciplinarity). This is very different from a structure with any elements whatever, it is an event of heterogeneous bodies, an event as such which crosses varied structures and specified sets. No longer is it a structure which frames isomorphic sets; it is an event which passes across irreducible domains. Take, for example, the 'catastrophe' event, studied by the mathematician René Thom. Or else the reproduction-event, 'to reproduce', which happens in a gel, but also in an epidemic or in a news item. Or else the TO MOVE ABOUT which can affect the course of a taxi in a town or of a fly in a swarm: this is not an axiom, but an event which is extended between qualified sets. They no longer extract a structure common to any elements whatever, they spread out an event, they countereffectuate an event which cuts different bodies and is effected in varied structures. There are, as it were, infinitive verbs, lines of becoming, lines which shoot between domains and leap from one domain to another, interregnums. Science will be increasingly like grass, in the middle, between things and between other things, accompanying their flight (it is true that the apparatus of power will increasingly demand a restoration of order, a recoding of science).

English humour (?), Jewish humour, Stoic humour, Zen humour: what a strange broken line. An ironist is someone who discusses principles; he is seeking a first principle, a principle which comes even before the one that was thought to be first, he finds a course which is even more primary than the others. He constantly goes up and down. This is why he proceeds by questioning, he is a man of conversation, of dialogue, he has a particular tone, always of the signifier. Humour is completely the opposite: principles count for little, everything is taken literally, the consequences are expected of you (this is why humour is not transmitted through plays on words, puns, which are of the signifier, and like a principle within the principle). Humour is the art of consequences or effects: OK, fine, you give me this? You'll see what happens. Humour is treacherous, it is treason. Humour is atonal, absolutely imperceptible, it makes something shoot off. It never goes up or down, it is on the surface: surface effects. Humour is an art of pure events. The arts of Zen, archery, gardening or taking tea, are exercises to make the event surge forth and dazzle on a pure surface. Jewish humour versus Greek irony, Job-humour versus Oedipus-irony, insular humour versus continental irony, Stoic humour versus Platonic irony, Zen humour versus Buddhist irony, masochist humour versus sadist irony, Proust-humour versus Gide-irony, etc. The whole destiny of irony is linked to representation, irony ensures the individuation of the represented or the subjectivation of the representer. Classical irony, in fact, consists in showing that what is most universal in representation is the same as the extreme individuality of the represented which serves as its principle (classical irony culminates in the theological affirmation according to which 'the whole of the possible' is at the same time the reality of God as singular being). Romantic irony, for its part, discovers the subjectivity of the principle of all possible representation. These problems are no concern of humour, which has always undermined games of principles or causes in favour of the event and games of individuation or subjectivation in favour of multiplicities. Irony contains an insufferable claim: that of belonging to a superior race, of being the preserve of the masters (a famous text of Renan says this without irony, for irony dries up quickly when talking of itself). Humour, on the other hand, claims kinship with a minority, with a minority-becoming. It is humour which makes a language stammer, which imposes on it a minor usage, or which constitutes a complete bilingual system within the same language. And, indeed, it never involves plays on words (there is not a single play on words in Lewis Carroll), but events of language, a minoritarian language, which has itself become creator of events. Or else, might there be 'indefinite' plays on words which would be like a becoming instead of a completion?

What is an assemblage? It is a multiplicity which is made up of many heterogeneous terms and which establishes liaisons, relations between them, across ages, sexes and reigns – different natures. Thus, the assemblage's only unity is that of co-functioning: it is a symbiosis, a 'sympathy'. It is never filiations which are important, but alliances, alloys; these are not successions, lines of descent, but contagions, epidemics, the wind. Magicians are well aware of this. An animal is defined less by its genus, its species, its organs, and its functions, than by the assemblages into which it enters. Take an assemblage of the type man-animal-manufactured object: MAN-HORSE-STIRRUP. Technologists have explained that the stirrup made possible a new military unity in giving the knight lateral stability: the lance could be tucked in under one arm, it benefits from all the horse's speed, acts as a point which is immobile itself but propelled by the gallop. 'The stirrup replaced the energy of man by the power of the animal.' This is a new man-animal symbiosis, a new assemblage of war, defined by its degree of power or 'freedom', its affects, its circulation of affects: what a set of bodies is capable of. Man and the animal enter into a new relationship, one changes no less than the other, the battlefield is filled with a new type of affects. It must not be thought, however, that the invention of the stirrup is sufficient. An assemblage is never technological; if anything, it is the opposite. Tools always presuppose a machine, and the machine is always social before being technical. There is always a social machine which selects or assigns the technical elements used. A tool remains marginal, or little used, until there exists a social machine or collective assemblage which is capable of taking it into its 'phylum'. In the case of the stirrup, it was the grant of land, linked to the beneficiary's obligation to serve on horseback, which was to impose the new cavalry and harness the tool in the complex assemblage of feudalism. (Formerly the stirrup had either been used, but used in another way, in the context of a completely different assemblage – for example, of nomads – or else it was known but not used, or used only in a very limited way, as in the battle of Adrianople.[20]) The feudal machine combines new relationships with the earth, war, the animal, but also with culture and games (tournaments), with woman (courtly love): all sorts of fluxes enter into conjunction. How can the assemblage be refused the name it deserves, 'desire'? Here desire becomes feudal. Here, as elsewhere, it is the set of the affects which are transformed and circulate in an assemblage of symbiosis, defined by the co-functioning of its heterogeneous parts.

First, in an assemblage there are, as it were, two faces, or at the least two heads. There are *states of things*, states of bodies (bodies interpenetrate, mix together, transmit affects to one another); but also *utterances*, regimes of utterances: signs are organized in a new way, new formulations appear, a new style for new gestures (the emblems which individualize the knight, the formulas of oaths, the system of 'declarations', even of love, etc.). Utterances are not part of ideology, there is no ideology: utterances, no less than states of things, are components and cog-wheels in the assemblage. There is no base or superstructure in an assemblage; a monetary flux in itself involves as many utterances as a flux of words, for its part, can involve money. Utterances are not content to describe corresponding states of things: these are rather, as it were, two non-parallel formalizations, the formalization of expression and the formalization of content, such that one never does what one says, one never says what one does, although one is not lying, one is not deceiving or being deceived, one is only assembling signs and bodies as heterogeneous components of the same machine. The only unity derives from the fact that one and the same function, one and the same 'functive', is the expressed of the utterance and the attribute of the state of body: an event which stretches out or contracts, a becoming in the infinitive. To feudalize? In an indissoluble way an assemblage is both machine assemblage of effectuation and collective assemblage of enunciation. In enunciation, in the production of utterances, there is no subject, but always collective agents: and in what the utterance speaks of there are no objects, but machinic states. These are like the variables of the function, which constantly interlace their values or their segments. No one has shown these two complementary faces of any assemblage more clearly than Kafka. If there is a Kafkaesque world, it is certainly not that of the strange or the absurd, but a world in which the most extreme juridicial formalization of utterances (questions and answers, objections, pleading, summing up, reasoned judgement, verdict), coexists with the most intense machinic formalization, the machinization of states of things and bodies (ship-machine, hotel-machine, circus-machine, castle-machine, lawsuit-machine). One and the same K-function, with its collective agents and bodily passions, Desire.

And then there is yet another axis along which assemblages must be divided. This time it is according to the movements which animate them, which determine or carry them along, which determine or carry along desire, with its states of things and utterances. There is no assemblage without territory, without territoriality and reterritorialization which includes all sorts of artifices. But is there any assemblage without a point of deterritorialization, without a line of flight which leads it on to new creations, or else towards death? Let us keep to the example of FEUDALISM. Feudal territorialities, or rather reterritorialization, since it is a case of a new distribution of land and a whole system of sub-infeudation; and does the knight not reterritorialize himself on his mount with stirrups, for he can sleep on his horse? But at the same time, either at the beginning or else towards the end, there is a vast movement of deterritorialization: deterritorialization of the empire and, above all, of the church, whose landed wealth is confiscated to be given to the knights. And this movement finds an outlet in the Crusades. However, in their turn, the Crusades bring about a reterritorialization of empire and church (the spiritual land, Christ's tomb, the new commerce); and the knight has always been inseparable from his wandering path, impelled by a wind, from his deterritorialization on horseback; and serfdom itself is inseparable from its feudal territoriality, but also from all the precapitalist deterritorializations with which it is already shot through.[21] The two movements coexist in an assemblage and yet are not equivalent, they do not balance out, are not symmetrical. We might say of the earth, or rather of the artificial reterritorialization which constantly takes place, that it gives a particular substance to the content, a particular code to the utterances, a particular limit to becoming, a particular indicative mood (present, past, future) to time. But it might be said that the deterritorialization which takes place at the same time – although from different points of view – does not affect the earth any less: it liberates a pure matter, it undoes codes, it carries expressions, contents, states of things and utterances along a zigzag broken line of flight, it raises time to the infinitive, it releases a becoming which no longer has any limit, because each term is a stop which must be jumped over. It always comes down to Blanchot's fine phrase: to release 'the part of the event which its accomplishment cannot realise': a pure dying or smiling or fighting or hating or loving or going away or creating ... A return to dualism? No, the two movements are caught up in each other, the assemblage arranges them both, everything happens between the two. Here again, there is a K-function, another axis which Kafka traced out in the dual movement of territorialities and deterritorialization.

There is indeed a historical question of the assemblage: particular heterogeneous elements caught in the function, the circumstances in which they are caught up, the set of relationships which at a particular moment unites man, animal, tools and environment. But man also never stops animal-becoming, tool-becoming, environment-becoming, according to another question within these very assemblages. Man only becomes animal if the animal, for its part, becomes sound, colour or line. It is a bloc of becoming which is always assymetrical. It is not that the two are exchanged, for they are not exchanged at all, but the one only becomes the other if the other becomes something yet other, and if the terms disappear. As Lewis Carroll says, it is when the smile is without a cat that man can effectively become cat as soon as he smiles. It is not man who sings or paints, it is man who becomes animal, but at exactly the same time as the animal becomes music, or pure colour, or an astonishingly simple line: with Mozart's birds it is the man who becomes a bird, because the bird becomes music. Melville's mariner becomes albatross when the albatross itself becomes extraordinary whiteness, pure vibration of white (and Captain Ahab's whale-becoming forms a bloc with Moby Dick's white-becoming, pure white wall). So is this it, to paint, to compose or to write? It is all a question of line, there is no substantial difference between painting, music and writing. These activities are differentiated from one another by their respective substances, codes and territorialities, but not by the abstract line they trace, which shoots between them and carries them towards a common fate. When we come to trace the line, we can say 'It is philosophy.' Not at all because philosophy would be an ultimate discipline, a last root, containing the truth of the others, on the contrary. Still less is it a popular wisdom. It is because philosophy is born or produced outside by the painter, the musician, the writer, each time that the melodic line draws along the sound, or the pure traced line colour, or the written line the articulated voice. There is no need for philosophy: it is necessarily produced where each activity gives rise to its line of deterritorialization. To get out of philosophy, to do never mind what so as to be able to produce it from outside. The philosophers have always been something else, they were born from something else.

Writing is very simple. Either it is a way of reterritorializing oneself, conforming to a code of dominant utterances, to a territory of established states of things: not just schools and authors, but all those who write professionally, even in a non-literary sense. Or else, on the other hand, it is becoming, becoming something other than a writer, since what one is becoming at the same time becomes something other than writing. Not every becoming passes through writing, but everything which becomes is an object of writing, painting or music. Everything which becomes is a pure line which ceases to represent whatever it may be. It is sometimes said that the novel reached its culminating point when it adopted an anti-hero as a character: an absurd, strange and disoriented creature who wanders about continually, deaf and blind. But this is the substance of the novel: from Beckett back to Chrétien de Troyes, from Lawrence back to Lancelot, passing through the whole history of the English and American novel. Chrétien de Troyes constantly traced the line of the wandering knights who sleep on horseback, supported by their lance and stirrups, who no longer know their name or destination, who constantly set off in zigzag line, who climb into the first cart to come along, even at the expense of their honour. The knight's point of deterritorialization. Sometimes in a feverish haste on the abstract line which carries them off, sometimes in the black hole of the catatonia which absorbs them. It is the wind, even a wind from the backyard, which sometimes hurries us along, sometimes immobilizes us. A KNIGHT TO SLEEP ON HIS HORSE. I am a poor lonesome cowboy.[22*] Writing has no other goal: wind, even when we do not move, 'keys in the wind to set my spirit to flight and give my thought a gust of air from the backyard' – to release what can be saved from life, that which can save itself by means of power and stubbornness, to extract from the event that which is not exhausted by the happening, to release from becoming that which will not permit itself to be fixed in a term. A strange ecology, tracing a line of writing, music or painting. These are ribbons stirred by the wind. A little air passes. A line is traced, the stronger for being abstract, if it is quite restrained, without figures. Writing is made of motor agitation and inertia: Kleist. It is true that one writes only for illiterates, for those who do not read or at least for those who will not read you. One writes always for animals, like Hofmannsthal who used to say that he felt a rat in his throat, and this used to show its teeth, 'nuptials or participation against nature', symbiosis, involution. Only the animal in man is addressed. This does not mean writing about one's dog, one's cat, one's horse or one's favourite animal. It does not mean making animals speak. It means writing as a rat traces a line, or as it twists its tail, as a bird sends out a sound, as a cat moves or else sleeps heavily. Animal-becoming, on condition that the animal, rat, horse, bird or cat, itself becomes something else, bloc, line, sound, colour of sand – an abstract line. For everything which changes passes along that line: assemblage. Being a sea-louse, which sometimes leaps up

metonymy. Psychoanalysis becomes more and more Ciceronian and Freud has always been a Roman. In order to renew the old distinction between true desire and false desire, psychoanalysis makes use of a grid which is perfect for the purpose: the true contents of desire would be partial drives [*pulsions partielles*] or partial objects; the true expression of desire would be Oedipus, or castration, or death – one instance to structure the whole. As soon as desire assembles [*agence*] something – in connection with an Outside, in connection with a becoming – the assemblage is broken up. As with fellatio: oral drive of sucking the breast + Oedipal structural accident. It's the same for everything else. Before psychoanalysis people used to talk about old men's revolting obsessions; with it, they talk about perverse childish activity.

We say, on the contrary: you haven't got hold of the unconscious, you never get hold of it, it is not an 'it was' in place of which the 'I' must come. The Freudian formula must be reversed. You have to produce the unconscious. It is not at all a matter of repressed memories or even of phantasms. You don't reproduce childhood memories, you produce blocs of child-becoming with *blocs of childhood* which are always in the present. A man manufactures or assembles [*agence*], not with the egg from which he emerged, nor with the progenitors who attach him to it, nor with the images that he draws from it, nor with the structure of germination, but with the scrap of placenta which he has hidden, and which is always contemporary with him, as raw material to experiment with. Produce some unconscious, and it is not easy, it is not just anywhere, not with a slip of the tongue, a pun or even a dream. The unconscious is a substance to be manufactured, to get flowing – a social and political space to be conquered. There is no subject of desire, any more than there is an object. There is no subject of enunciation. Fluxes are the only objectivity of desire itself. Desire is the system of a-signifying signs with which fluxes of the unconscious are produced in a social field. There is no blossoming of desire, wherever it happens – in an unremarkable family or a local school – which does not call established structures into question. Desire is revolutionary because it always wants more connections and assemblages. But psychoanalysis cuts off and beats down all connections, all assemblages – it hates desire, it hates politics. The second criticism concerns the way in which psychoanalysis prevents the formation of utterances. Assemblages – in their content – are populated by becomings and intensities, by intensive circulations, by various multiplicities (packs, masses, species, races, populations, tribes . . .). And in their expression, assemblages handle indefinite articles or pronouns which are not at all indeterminate ('a' tummy, 'some' people, 'one' hits 'a' child . . .) – verbs in the infinitive which are not undifferentiated but which mark processes (to walk, to kill, to love . . .) – proper names which are not people but events (they can be groups, animals, entities, singularities, collectives, everything that is written with a capital letter, A-HANS-BECOMING-HORSE). The collective machine assemblage is a material production of desire as well as an expressive cause of utterance: a semiotic articulation of chains of expressions whose contents are relatively the least formalized. Not representing a subject – for there is no subject of enunciation – but programming an assemblage. Not overcoding utterances but, on the contrary, preventing them from toppling under the tyranny of supposedly significant combinations. Now, it is curious that psychoanalysis – which boasts that it has so much logic – understands nothing of the logic of the indefinite article, of the infinitive of the verb and of the proper name. The psychoanalyst wants there to be, at all costs, a definite, a possessive, a personal, hidden behind the indefinite. When Melanie Klein's children say 'a tummy' or ask 'How do people grow up?', Melanie Klein hears 'my mummy's tummy' or 'Will I be big like my daddy?' When they say 'a Hitler', 'a Churchill', Melanie Klein sees here the possessive of the bad mother or of the good father. Military men and weathermen –

more than psychoanalysts – have at least got the sense of the
proper name when they use it to refer to a strategic operation or
geographical process: Operation Typhoon. On one occasion
Jung tells Freud about one of his dreams: he has dreamed of an
ossuary. Freud wants Jung to have desired someone's death,
doubtless that of his wife. 'Surprised, Jung pointed out to him
that there were several skulls, not just one.'[1] In the same way,
Freud does not want there to be six or seven wolves: there will
only be one representative of the father. And again, there is what
Freud does with little Hans: he takes no account of the
assemblage   (building-street-nextdoor-warehouse-omnibus-
horse-a-horse-falls-a-horse-is-whipped!); he takes no account of
the situation (the child had been forbidden to go into the street,
etc.); he takes no account of little Hans's endeavour (horse-
becoming, because every other way out has been blocked up: the
childhood bloc, the bloc of Hans's animal-becoming, the infinitive as marker of a becoming, the line of flight or the
movement of deterritorialization). The only important thing for
Freud is that the horse be the father – and that's the end of it. In
practice, given an assemblage, extracting a segment from it,
abstracting a moment from it, is sufficient to break up the
ensemble of desire, to break up becoming in act [*le devenir en acte*],
and to substitute for them over-imaginary resemblances (a horse
= my daddy) or analogies of over-symbolic relationships (to
buck = to make love). All the real-desire has already dis-
appeared: a code is put in its place, a symbolic overcoding of
utterances, a fictitious subject of enunciation who doesn't give
the patients a chance.

   If you go to be psychoanalysed, you believe that you will be
able to talk and because of this belief you accept the need to pay.
But you don't have the least chance of talking. Psychoanalysis is
entirely designed to prevent people from talking and to remove
from them all conditions of true enunciation. We have formed a
small working group for the following task: to read reports of
psychoanalysis, especially of children; to stick exclusively to
these reports and make two columns, on the left what the child

said, according to the account itself, and on the right what the psychoanalyst heard and retained (cf. always the card trick of the 'forced choice'). It's horrifying. The two central texts in this respect are Freud's little Hans and Melanie Klein's little Richard. It's an amazing forcing,[2*] like a boxing match between categories which are too unequal. At the outset there is Richard's humour, which makes fun of M.K. All these assemblages of desire on his part pass through a mapping activity during the war: a distribution of proper names, of territorialities and deterritorializing movements, thresholds and crossings. Insensitive and deaf, impervious, Mrs K. is going to break little Richard's strength. The leitmotif of the book is in the text itself: 'Mrs K. interpreted, Mrs K. *interpreted*, Mrs K. INTERPRETED . . .' It is said that there is no longer any of this today: signifiance has replaced interpretation, the signifier has replaced the signified, the analyst's silence has replaced the commentaries, castration is revealed to be more certain than Oedipus, structural functions have replaced parental images, the name of the Father has replaced my daddy. We see no important practical changes. A patient cannot mutter 'mouths of the Rhône' [*bouches du Rhône*] without being corrected – 'mother's mouth' [*bouche de la mère*]; another cannot say, 'I would like to join a hippie group' [*groupe hippie*] without being asked 'Why do you pronounce it big pee?' [*gros pipi*]. These two examples form part of analyses based on the highest signifier. And what could analysis consist of, if not these kind of things about which the analyst no longer even needs to talk because the person analysed knows them as well as he does? The person analysed has therefore become the analyser – a particularly comic term. It's all very well to say to us: you understand nothing, Oedipus, it's not daddy-mummy, it's the symbolic, the law, the arrival at culture, it's the effect of the signifier, it's the finitude of the subject, it has the 'lack-to-be[3*] which is life'. And if it's not Oedipus, it will be castration, and the supposed death drives. Psychoanalysts teach infinite resignation, they are the last priests (no, there will be others after them). It cannot be said that they are very jolly; see the dead look they have, their stiff necks (only Lacan has kept a certain sense of laughter, but he admits that he is forced to laugh alone). They are right to say that they need to be 'remunerated' to put up with the burden of what they hear; they have none the less given up supporting the thesis of a symbolic and disinterested role for money in psychoanalysis. We open by chance some article by an authoritative psychoanalyst, a two-page article: 'Man's long dependence, his powerlessness to help himself . . . the human being's congenital inferiority . . . the narcissistic wound inherent in his existence . . . the painful reality of the human condition . . . which implies incompletion, conflict . . . his intrinsic misery, which it is true leads him to the most elevated creations.' A priest would have been long since hounded out of his church for sustaining so insolent and obscurantist a style.

But yes, nevertheless, many things have changed in psychoanalysis. Either it has swamped, it is spread into all sorts, of techniques of therapy, of adjustment or even marketing, to which it brought its particular touch in a vast syncretism, its little line in group polyphony. Or it has hardened, in a refinement, a very lofty 'return' to Freud, a solitary harmony, a triumphant specifying that wants no more pacts except with linguistics (even if the reverse is not true). But whatever their considerable difference, we believe that these two opposed directions provide evidence of the same changes, of the same evolution, which bears on several points.

(1) First, psychoanalysis has displaced its centre – from the family to married life. It sets itself up between spouses, lovers or friends rather than between parents and children. Even children are guided by psychologists rather than being led along by their parents – or parent-child relations are regulated by radio consultations. The phantasm has made childhood memory redundant. This is a practical remark, which bears on the recruitment of people to be psychoanalysed: this recruitment takes place less and less according to the genealogy

of the family tree and more and more according to the circle of friends ('You ought to get analysed as well'). As Serge Leclaire says, perhaps humorously, 'there are now analyses where the circles of allegiance of couches frequented by friends and lovers take the place of relations of kinship'.[4] This is of some importance to the actual form of problems: neurosis has abandoned hereditary models (even if heredity moves through a family milieu) to pursue patterns of contagion. Neurosis has acquired its most frightening power, that of propagation by contagion: 'I will not let go of you until you have joined me in this condition.' We admire the discretion of the earlier neurotics, of the hysterics or obsessionals, who either got on with their business alone or did it in the family: the modern depressive types are, on the contrary, particularly vampiric or poisonous. They take it on themselves to bring about Nietzsche's prophecy: they cannot bear the existence of 'a' health; they will constantly draw us into their clutches. Yet to cure them would mean first destroying this will to venom in them. But how could the psychoanalyst do this – the same man who derives from it an excellent self-recruitment of his clientele? It might have been thought that May 68 would have dealt a mortal blow to psychoanalysis and would have made the style of specifically psychoanalytic utterances seem absurd. No, so many young people have returned to psychoanalysis. Precisely because it was able to abandon its discredited family model in order to take up a still more worrying direction, a 'political' micro-contagion instead of a 'private' macro-lineage. Never has psychoanalysis been so full of life, whether because it has succeeded in penetrating everything, or because it has established new foundations for its transcendent position, its specific Order.

(2) Historically, psychiatry does not seem to us to have been constituted around the notion of madness but, on the contrary, at the point where this notion proved difficult to apply. Psychiatry essentially ran up against the problem of cases of delirium where the intellectual faculty was intact. On

the one hand, there are people who seem to be mad, but who are not 'really' so, having kept their faculties, and first and foremost the faculty of properly managing their money and their possessions (paranoid conduct, the delirium of interpretation, etc.).[5] On the other hand, there are people who are 'really' mad and yet don't seem to be, suddenly committing an outrageous act which nothing led us to foresee, arson, murder, etc. (monomaniac conduct, the delirium of passion or revenge). If the psychiatrist has a bad conscience, it is because he has had one since the outset, because he is implicated in the dissolution of the notion of madness: he is accused of treating as insane certain people who are not exactly so, and of not seeing in time the madness of others who clearly are. Psychoanalysis slipped between these two poles, saying that we were at once all insane without seeming to be, but also that we seemed mad without being so. A whole 'psychopathology of everyday life'. In short, it is around the failure of the notion of madness that psychiatry is constituted and that psychoanalysis has been able to link up with it. It is difficult to add anything to the analyses first of Foucault, then of Robert Castel, when they show how psychoanalysis has grown in the soil of psychiatry.[6] By discovering between the two poles the world of neurotics, their intellectual faculties intact, and even absence of delirium, psychoanalysis, at its inception, succeeded in bringing off a very important manoeuvre: getting all sorts of people to go through the liberal contractual relationship who had until then seemed excluded from it ('madness' put all those it afflicted outside all possible contracts). The specifically psychoanalytic contract, a flux of words for a flux of money, was going to make the psychoanalyst someone able to insert himself into every pore of the society occupied by these doubtful cases. But the more psychoanalysis saw it was gaining ground, the more it turned towards the deliriums concealed behind neuroses, the less it seems to have been happy with the contractual relationship – even if, on the face of it, it was retained. Psychoanalysis had in fact achieved what was the source of Freud's anxiety at the end of his life; it had become interminable, interminable in principle. At the same time, it assumed a 'mass' function. For what defines a mass function is not necessarily a collective, class or group character; it is the juridical transition from contract to statute. It seems more and more that psychoanalysis is acquiring an untransferable, inalienable, *statutory fixity*, rather than entering into a temporary *contractual relationship*. Precisely by setting itself up between the two poles where psychiatry came up against its limits, by enlarging the field between these two poles and exploring it, psychoanalysis was to invent a statute law of mental illness or psychic difficulty which constantly renewed itself and spread out into a systematic network. A new ambition was being offered to us: psychoanalysis is a lifelong affair.

The importance of the Ecole Freudienne de Paris is perhaps particularly connected to the fact that it expressed for the first time the requirements of a new psychoanalytic order, not just in theory, but in its statutory organization, in its founding acts. For what it clearly proposes is a psychoanalytic statute, in opposition to the old contract: at a stroke it envisages a bureaucratic mutation, the transition from a bureaucracy of the eminent (the radical-socialist type, which suited the beginnings of psychoanalysis) to a mass bureaucracy; this time an ideal of giving out statutory documents like certificates of citizenship, identity cards, in contrast to limited contracts. Psychoanalysis invokes Rome, assumes a Ciceronian air and sets up its boundary between 'Honestas' and 'the rabble'.[7] If the Ecole Freudienne has brought so many problems to the psychoanalytic world, it is not simply as a result of its theoretical hauteur or of its practice, but because of its plan for a new explicit organization. The other psychoanalytic bodies may have judged this project to be inappropriate; but they did so because it told the truth about a change which affects the whole of psychoanalysis and which the other organizations preferred silently to leave alone, under the cover of the contractual motif. We do not regret the passing of this contractual cover-up which was hypocritical from the start. Moreover, we are not saying that psychoanalysis is now concerned with the masses, but simply that it has assumed a mass function – whether this was phantasmal or restricted, or for an 'élite'. And this is the second aspect of its change: not only to have moved from family to conjugality, from kinship to match, from lineage to contagion, but also from *contract to statute*. On occasion the interminable years of psychoanalysis give social workers additional 'salary increments'; psychoanalysis can be seen permeating every part of the social sector.[8] This seems to us to be more important than the practice and the theory which in general outline have stayed the same. Hence the reversal of the relations between psychoanalysis and psychiatry, hence psychoanalysis' ambition to become an official language; hence its pacts with linguistics (we do not have a contractual relationship with language).

(3) Yet the theory itself has changed, seems to have changed. The transition from the signified to the signifier: if we no longer look for a signified for supposedly significant symptoms; if we look, on the contrary, for the signifier for symptoms which would be no more than its effect; if interpretation gives way to signifiance – then a new shift takes place. Psychoanalysis then has, in effect, its own references and has no more use for an external 'referent'. Everything that happens in psychoanalysis in the analyst's consulting room is true. What happens elsewhere is derived or secondary. An excellent method for encouraging trust. Psychoanalysis has ceased to be an experimental science in order to get hold of an axiomatic system. Psychoanalysis, *index sui*; no other truth than that which emerges from the operation which presupposes it; the couch has become the bottomless well, interminable in principle. Psychoanalysis has stopped being 'in search of' because it is now constitutive of truth. Once again, it is Serge Leclaire who puts it most succinctly: 'The reality of

the primitive scene tends to reveal itself more concretely by means of the analytic consulting room than in the surroundings of the parental bedroom . . . From a figurative version, we move to the version of reference, a structural one, revealing the reality of a literal manoeuvre . . . The psychoanalysts couch has become the place where the game of confronting the real properly unfolds.' The psychoanalyst has become like the journalist: he creates the event. At any rate, psychoanalysis advertises its wares. So long as it interpreted or so long as it interprets (search for a signified), it returns desires and utterances to a condition which is deviant by comparison with the established order, by comparison with dominant meanings, but by the same token localizes them in the pores of this dominant, established body, like something which can be translated and exchanged by virtue of a contract. When it discovers the signifier, it appeals to a specifically psychoanalytic order (the symbolic order in opposition to the imaginary order of the signified), whose only need is itself, because it is statutory or structural: it is it which develops a body, a corpus sufficient by itself.

Once again we clearly come up against the question of power, of the apparatus of psychoanalytic power – with the same inflections as before: even if this power is narrow, localized, etc. This question can only be posed in terms of very general remarks: it is true, as Foucault says, that every formation of power needs a form of knowledge which, while not dependent on it, would itself lack all effectiveness without it. Now this usable knowledge may take two shapes: either an unofficial form, so that it can set itself up in the 'pores', to seal some hole or other in the established order; or an official form, when it itself constitutes a symbolic order which gives a generalized axiomatic system to the established powers. For example, the historians of antiquity show the complementarity of Greek city and Euclidean geometry. It was not because the geometricians had power but because Euclidean geometry constituted the knowledge, or the abstract machine, that the city needed for its organization of power, space and time. There is no State which does not need an image of thought which will serve as its axiomatic system or abstract machine, and to which it gives in return the strength to function: hence the inadequacy of the concept of ideology, which in no way takes into account this relationship. This was the unhappy role of classical philosophy – as we have seen it – that of supplying, in this way, the apparatuses of power, Church and State, with the knowledge which suited them. Could we say today that the human sciences have assumed this same role, that of providing by their own methods an abstract machine for modern apparatuses of power – receiving from them valuable endorsement in return? So psychoanalysis has submitted its tender, to become a major official language and knowledge in place of philosophy; to provide an axiomatic system of man in place of mathematics; to invoke the Honestas and a mass function. It is doubtful whether it is succeeding: the apparatuses of power have more interest in turning to physics, biology or informatics. But psychoanalysis will have done what it could: it no longer serves the established order unofficially: it offers a specific and symbolic order, an abstract machine, an official language that it tries to weld on to linguistics in general, to assume a position of Invariant. It is more and more concerned with pure 'thought'. Living psychoanalysis. Dead psychoanalysis, because it has little chance of succeeding in its ambition, because there are too many competitors and because, at the present time, all the forces of minority, all the forces of becoming, all the forces of language, all the forces of art, are in the process of fleeing from this particular ground – in the process of talking, thinking, acting and becoming in other ways. Everything is happening by another route which psychoanalysis can't even intercept, or which psychoanalysis only intercepts in order to stop. And this is the very task which it sets itself: to overcode assemblages in order to subject desires to signifying chains, utterances to the status of subjective examples – all of which

reconcile them with an established Order. The four pro-
gressive changes that we have just seen – transition from the
family to the circle of contacts, substitution of statute for
contract, discovery of a specifically psychoanalytic order, a
pact with linguistics – mark this ambition to take part in the
regulation of assemblages of desire and of enunciation, or even
to stake out a dominant position in this regulation.

We have been credited with many blunders about the
Anti-Oedipus, about desiring machines, about what an
assemblage of desire is, the forces that it mobilizes, the
dangers it confronts. They did not come from us. We said that
desire is in no sense connected to the 'Law' and cannot be
defined by any fundamental lack. For that's the real idea of
the priest: the constituent law at the heart of desire, desire
constituted as lack, the holy castration, the split subject, the
death drive, the strange culture of death. And it is doubtless
like this each time that desire is conceived as a bridge between
a subject and an object: the subject of desire cannot but be
split, and the object lost in advance. What we tried to show,
on the contrary, was how desire was beyond these person-
ological or objectal co-ordinates. It seemed to us that desire
was a process and that it unrolled a *plane of consistence*, a field of
immanence, a 'body without organs', as Artaud put it, criss-
crossed by particles and fluxes which break free from objects
and subjects . . . Desire is therefore not internal to a subject,
any more than it tends towards an object: it is strictly immanent to a plane which it does not pre-exist, to a plane which
must be constructed, where particles are emitted and fluxes
combine. There is only desire in so far as there is deployment
of a particular field, propagation of particular fluxes, emission
of particular particles. Far from presupposing a subject, desire
cannot be attained except at the point where someone is
deprived of the power of saying 'I'. Far from directing itself
towards an object, desire can only be reached at the point
where someone no longer searches for or grasps an object any
more than he grasps himself as subject. The objection is then

made that such a desire is totally indeterminate, and that it is even more imbued with lack. But who has you believe that by losing the co-ordinates of object and subject you lack something? Who is pushing you into believing that indefinite articles and pronouns (a, one), third persons (he, she) and verbs in the infinitive are in the least indeterminate? The plane of consistence or of immanence, the body without organs, includes voids and deserts. But these are 'fully' part of desire, far from accentuating some kind of lack in it. What a strange confusion – that of void with lack. We really do lack in general a particle of the East, a grain of Zen. Anorexia is perhaps the thing about which most wrong has been spoken – particularly under the influence of psychoanalysis. The void which is specific to the anorexic body without organs has nothing to do with a lack, and is part of the constitution of the field of desire criss-crossed by particles and fluxes. We will shortly return to this example to give more detail. But already the desert is a body without organs which has never been hostile to the groups who people it; the void has never been hostile to the particles which move about in it.

We have an image of the desert which involves the thirsty explorer, and an image of the void, as a ground which opens up. Images related to death which are only valid where the plane of consistence, which is identical to desire, is unable to establish itself and does not have the conditions to build on. But, on the plane of consistence, even the scarcity of particles and the slowing down and drying up of fluxes are part of desire, and of the pure life of desire, without indicating any lack. As Lawrence says, chastity is a flux. Is the plane of consistence something very strange? We would have to say simultaneously not only: 'You've got it already, you do not feel desire without its being already there, without its being mapped out at the same time as your desire', but also: 'You haven't got it, and you don't desire it if you can't manage to construct it, if you don't know how to, by finding your places, your assemblages, your particles and your fluxes.' We would have to say simultaneously not only: 'It is created all alone, but know how to see it', and also: 'You have to create it, know how to create it, take the right directions, at your risk and peril.' Desire: who, except priests, would want to call it 'lack'? Nietzsche called it 'Will to Power'. There are other names for it. For example, 'grace'. Desiring is not at all easy, but this is precisely because it gives, instead of lacks, 'virtue which gives'. Those who link desire to lack, the long column of crooners of castration, clearly indicate a long resentment, like an interminable bad conscience. Is this to misunderstand the misery of those who really do lack something? But apart from the fact that psychoanalysis does not talk about these people (on the contrary, it makes the distinction, it says pompously enough that it is not concerned with real privations), those whose lack is real have no possible plane of consistence which would allow them to desire. They are prevented from doing this in a thousand ways. And as soon as they construct one, they lack nothing on this plane, and from this starting-point they set off victoriously towards that which they lack outside. Lack refers to a positivity of desire, and not the desire to a negativity of lack. Even individually, the construction of the plane is a politics, it necessarily involves a 'collective', collective assemblages, a set of social becomings.

We should distinguish between two planes, two types of planes. On the one hand, a plane that could be called one of *organization*. It concerns both the development of forms and the formation of subjects. It is therefore, as much as one wishes, structural *and* genetic. In any case, it possesses a supplementary dimension, one dimension more, a hidden dimension, since it is not given for itself, but must always be concluded, inferred, induced on the basis of what it organizes. It is like in music where the principle of composition is not given in a directly perceptible, audible, relation with what it provides. It is therefore a plane of transcendence, a kind of design, in the mind of man or in the mind of a god, even when it is accorded a maximum of immanence by plunging it into the depths of Nature, or of the Unconscious. One such plane is that of the Law, in so far as it organizes and develops forms, genres, themes, motifs, and assigns and causes the evolution of subjects, persons, characteristic features and feelings: harmony of forms, education of subjects.

And then there is a completely different plane which does not deal with these things: the plane of Consistence. This other plane knows only relations of movement and rest, of speed and slowness, between unformed, or relatively unformed, elements, molecules or particles borne away by fluxes. It knows nothing of subjects, but rather what are called 'hecceities'.[9]* In fact no individuation takes place in the manner of a subject or even of a thing. An hour, a day, a season, a climate, one or several years – a degree of heat, an intensity, very different intensities which combine – have a perfect individuality which should not be confused with that of a thing or of a formed subject. 'What a terrible five o'clock in the afternoon!' It is not the moment, and it is not brevity, which distinguishes this type of individuation. A hecceity can last as long as, and even longer than, the time required for the development of a form and the evolution of a subject. But it is not the same kind of time: floating times, the floating lines of Aion as distinct from Chronos. Hecceities are simply degrees of power which combine, to which correspond a power to affect and be affected, active or passive affects, intensities. On her stroll Virginia Woolf's heroine penetrates like a blade through all things, and yet looks from the outside, with the impression that it is dangerous to live even a single day ('Never again will I say: I am this or that, he is this, he is that . . .'). But the stroll is itself a hecceity. It is hecceities that are being expressed in indefinite, but not indeterminate, articles and pronouns; in proper names which do not designate people but mark events, in verbs in the infinitive which are not undifferentiated but constitute becomings or processes. It is hecceity which needs this kind of enunciation. HECCEITY = EVENT. It is a question of life, to live in this way, on the basis of such a plane, or rather on such a plane: *'He is as lawless as the wind and very secret about what he does at night'* (Charlotte Brontë). Where does the absolute perfection of this sentence come from? Pierre Chevalier is moved by this sentence which he discovers and which runs through him; would he be moved if he was not himself a hecceity which runs through the sentence? A thing, an animal, a person are now only definable by movements and rests, speeds and slownesses (*longitude*) and by affects, intensities (*latitude*).[10] There are no more forms but cinematic relations between unformed elements; there are no more subjects but dynamic individuations without subjects, which constitute collective assemblages. Nothing develops, but things arrive late or in advance, and enter into some assemblage according to their compositions of speed. Nothing becomes subjective but hecceities take shape according to the compositions of non-subjective powers and effects. Map of speeds and intensities. We have already encountered this business of speeds and slownesses: their common quality is to grow from the middle, to be always-in-between; they have in common the imperceptible, like the vast slowness of massive Japanese wrestlers, and all of a sudden, a decisive gesture so swift that we didn't see it. Speed has no privilege over slowness: both fray the nerves, or rather, train them and give them mastery. Antoine. What is a young girl or a group of young girls? Proust describes them as moving relationships of slowness and speed, and individuations by hecceity which are not subjective.

It is this plane, defined uniquely by longitude and latitude, which may be opposed to the plane of organization. It is truly a plane of immanence because it possesses no dimension supplementary to what occurs on it; its dimensions grow or decrease with what occurs on it, without its planitude being endangered (plane with n dimensions). This is no longer a teleological plane, a design, but a geometrical plane, an abstract drawing, which is like the section of all the various forms, whatever their dimensions. Planomenon or Rhizosphere, hypersphere. It is like a fixed plane, but 'fixed' does not mean motionless; it indicates the absolute state of movement as well as that of rest, in relation to which all variations in relative speed themselves become perceptible. This plane of immanence or consistence includes fogs, plagues, voids, jumps, immobilizations, suspensions, hastes. For being thwarted is a part of the plane itself: we always have to start again, start again from the middle, to give the elements new relations of speed and slowness which make them change assemblage, jump from one assemblage to another. Hence the multiplicity of planes on the plane, and the voids which form part of the plane, as a silence forms part of a plane of sound [*plan sonore*], without it being possible to say 'something is missing'. Boulez speaks of 'programming the machine so each time a track is replayed, it gives different characteristics of tempo'. And Cage speaks of a clock that would give variable speeds. Some contemporary musicians have pushed to the limit the practical idea of an immanent plane which no longer has a hidden principle of organization, but where the process must be heard no less than what comes out of it; where forms are only retained to set free variations of speed between particles or molecules of sound; where themes, motifs and subjects are only retained to set free floating affects. The extraordinary way in which Boulez deals with the Wagnerian leitmotif. It would not be enough to oppose the East and the West here, the plane of immanence which comes from the East and the plane of transcendent organization which was always the disease of the West; for example, eastern poetry or drawing, the martial arts, which so often proceed by pure hecceities and grow from the 'middle'. The West itself is criss-crossed by this immense plane of immanence or of consistence, which carries off forms and strips them of their indications of speed, which dissolve subjects and extract their hecceities, nothing left but longitudes and latitudes.

Plane of consistence, plane of immanence – Spinoza already conceived the plane in this way in opposition to the supporters of order and law, philosophers or theologians. The trinity Hölderlin–Kleist–Nietzsche already conceived writing, art and even a new politics in this way: no longer as a harmonious development of form and a well-ordered formation of the subject, as Goethe or Schiller or Hegel wanted, but successions of catatonic states and periods of extreme haste, of suspensions and shootings, coexistences of variable speeds, blocs of becoming, leaps across voids, displacements of a centre of gravity on an abstract line, conjunctions of lines on a plane of immanence, a 'stationary process' at dizzying speed which sets free particles and affects. (Two secrets of Nietzsche: the eternal return as fixed plane selecting the always variable speeds and slownesses of Zarathustra; the aphorism not as writing in small pieces, but as assemblage which cannot be read twice, which cannot 'replay' without changing the speeds and slownesses between its elements.) It is all that, it is all this plane which has only one name – Desire – and which has absolutely nothing to do with lack or with the 'law'. As Nietzsche says, who would want to call this law? – the word has too much of a moral aftertaste.

So we were saying a simple thing: desire concerns speeds and slownesses between particles (longitude), affects, intensities and hecceities in degrees of power (latitude). A – VAMPIRE – TO SLEEP – DAY – AND – TO WAKE UP – NIGHT. Do you realize how simple a desire is? Sleeping is a desire. Walking is a desire. Listening to music, or making music, or writing, are desires. A spring, a winter, are desires. Old age also is a desire. Even death. Desire never needs interpreting, it is it which experiments. Then we run up against very exasperating objections. They say to us that we are returning to an old cult of pleasure, to a pleasure principle, or to a notion of the festival (the revolution will be a festival . . .). By way of objection they hold up those who are stopped from sleeping, whether for internal or external reasons, and who have neither the means nor the time for a festival; or who have neither the time nor the culture to listen to music; nor the ability to walk, nor to go into a catatonic state except in hospital; or who are suddenly struck by a horrible old age or death, in short all those who suffer: don't they 'lack' something? And above all, it is objected that by releasing desire from lack and law, the only thing we have left to refer to is a state of nature, a desire which would be natural and spontaneous reality. We say quite the opposite: *desire only exists when assembled or machined.* You cannot grasp or conceive of a desire outside a determinate assemblage, on a plane which is not pre-existent but which must itself be constructed. All that is important is that each group or individual should construct the plane of immanence on which they lead their life and carry on their business. Without these conditions you obviously do lack something, but you lack precisely the conditions which make a desire possible. Organizations of forms, formations of subjects (the other plane), 'incapacitate' desire: they subjugate it to law and introduce lack into it. If you tie someone up and say to him 'Express yourself, friend', the most he will be able to say is that he doesn't want to be tied up. The only spontaneity in desire is doubtless of that kind: to not want to be oppressed, exploited, enslaved, subjugated. But no desire has ever been created with non-wishes. Not to want to be enslaved is a non-proposition. In retrospect every assemblage expresses and creates a desire by constructing the plane which makes it possible and, by making it possible, brings it about. Desire is not restricted to the privileged; neither is it restricted to the success of a revolution once it has occurred. It is in itself an immanent revolutionary process. *It is constructivist, not at all spontaneist.* Since every assemblage is collective, is itself a collective, it is indeed true that every desire is the affair of the people, or an affair of the masses, a molecular affair.

We don't even believe in internal drives which would prompt desire. The plane of immanence has nothing to do with an interiority; it is like the Outside where all desires come from. When we hear of a thing as stupid as the supposed death drive, it is like seeing a shadow theatre, Eros and Thanatos. We have to ask: could there be an assemblage so warped, so hideous, that the utterance 'Long live death' would be an actual part of it and death itself be desired in it? Or isn't this the opposite of an assemblage, its downfall, its failure? We must describe the assemblage in which such a desire becomes possible, gets moving and declares itself. But never will we point to drives which would refer to structural invariants, or to genetic variables. Oral, anal, genital, etc.: we ask each time into which assemblages these components enter, not to which drives they correspond, nor to which memories or fixations they owe their importance, nor to which incidents they refer, but with which extrinsic elements they combine to create a desire, to create desire. This is already the case with children who fabricate their desire with the outside, with the conquest of the outside, not in internal stages or by transcendent structures. Once again little Hans: there is the street, the horse, the omnibus, the parents, Professor Freud himself, the 'has a pee' [*fait-pipi*] which is neither an organ nor a function, but a machine function, one of the parts of the machine. There are speeds and slownesses, affects and hecceities: a horse a day the street. There are only different politics of assemblages, even with children: in this sense everything is political. There are only programmes, or rather diagrams or planes, not memories or even phantasms. There are only becomings and blocs, childhood blocs, blocs of femininity, of animality, blocs of present becoming, and nothing of the memorial, the imaginary or the symbolic. Desire is no more symbolic than figurative, no more signified than signifier: it is made up of different lines which cross, articulate or impede each other and which constitute a particular assemblage on a plane of immanence. But the plane does not pre-exist these assemblages which comprise it, these abstract lines which map it out. We can always call it plane of Nature, in order to underline its immanence. But the nature –artifice distinction is not at all relevant here. There is no desire which does not result in the coexistence of several levels, some of which can be called natural in contrast to others; but this is a nature which must be constructed with all the fabrications of the plane of immanence. The assemblage of feudalism includes among its elements 'horse-stirrup-lance'. The natural position of the knight, the natural way of holding the lance, depends on a new symbiosis of man-animal which makes the stirrup the most natural thing in the world and the horse the most artificial one. The figures of desire do not derive from this, but were already mapping out the assemblage, the set of elements, retained or created by the assemblage, the Lady no less than the horse, the sleeping knight no less than the wandering quest for the Grail.

We say that there is assemblage of desire each time that there are produced, in a field of immanence, or on a plane of consistence, *continuums of intensities, combinations of fluxes, emissions of particles* at variable speeds. Guattari speaks of a Schumann-assemblage. What is a musical assemblage like this, designated by a proper name? What are the dimensions of such an assemblage? There is the relationship with Clara, woman-child-virtuoso, the Clara line. There is the little manual machine that Schumann puts together to hold the middle finger tight and secure the independence of the fourth finger. There is the ritornello, the little ritornellos which haunt Schumann and run through all his work like so many childhood blocs, a whole concerted enterprise of involution, restraint and exhaustion of the theme and form. And there is also the use of the piano, this movement of deterritorialization which carries away the ritornello ('wings have sprouted on the child') on a melodic line, in an original polyphonic assemblage capable of producing dynamic and affective relations of speed or slowness, of delay or anticipation which are very complex, on the basis of an intrinsically simple or simplified form. There is the intermezzo, or rather there is

nothing but intermezzi in Schumann, making the music pass
to the middle preventing the sound plane from toppling under a
law of organization or development.[11] All of this is articulated
in the constitutive assemblage of desire. It is desire itself
which passes and moves. There is no need to be Schumann.
Listen to Schumann. Conversely, there is what happens to
make the whole assemblage waver: the little manual machine
leads to paralysis of the finger, and then to Schumann's
mad-becoming . . . We simply say that desire is inseparable
from a plane of consistence which must be constructed every
time piece by piece and from assemblages on this plane,
continuums, combinations, emissions. Without lack, but de-
finitely not without risk or peril. Desire, says Félix: a
ritornello. But this is already very complicated: for the
ritornello is a kind of sound territoriality, the child reassuring
himself when he is afraid in the dark, 'Rockabye baby on the
tree-top' . . .[12*] (Psychoanalysis seriously misunderstood the
famous 'Fort-Da' when it saw in it an opposition of a
phonological kind instead of recognizing a ritornello.) But it is
also the whole movement of deterritorialization which takes
hold of a form and a subject to extract from them variable
speeds and floating affects; then the music begins. What
counts in desire is not the false alternative of law–spontaneity,
nature–artifice; it is the respective play of territorialities, reterritorializations and movements of deterritorialization.

In speaking of desire we were no longer thinking of pleasure
and its festivals. Certainly pleasure is agreeable; certainly we
move towards it with all our might. But in its most attractive
and indispensable forms, it comes rather as an interruption in
the process of desire as constitution of a field of immanence.
There is nothing more revealing than the idea of a pleasure-
discharge; once pleasure is attained, one would have a little
calm before desire is rekindled: there is a lot of hatred, or fear,
of desire, in the cult of pleasure. Pleasure is the attribution of
the affect, the affection for a person or subject, it is the only
means for a person to 'find himself again' in the process of

desire which overwhelms him. Pleasures, even the most artificial, or the dizziest, can only be reterritorialization. Desire does not have pleasure as its norm, but this is not in the name of an internal Lack which could not be filled, but on the contrary by virtue of its positivity; that is, of the plane of consistence that it traces in the course of its process. It is the same error which relates desire to the Law of the lack and to the Norm of pleasure. It is when you keep relating desire to pleasure, to the attainment of pleasure, that you also notice that something fundamental is missing. To the point where, to break these preformed alliances between desire-pleasure-lack, we are obliged to make detours through bizarre fabrications, with much ambiguity. Take, as an example, courtly love, which is an assemblage of desire connected to feudalism as end. Dating an assemblage is not doing history, it is giving the assemblage its co-ordinates of expression and content, proper names, infinitive-becomings, articles, hecceities. (So that's what doing history is?) Now, it is well known that courtly love implies tests which postpone pleasure, or at least postpone the ending of coitus. This is certainly not a method of deprivation. It is the constitution of a field of immanence, where desire constructs its own plane and lacks nothing, any more than it allows itself to be interrupted by a discharge which would indicate that it is too heavy for it to bear. Courtly love has two enemies which merge into one: a religious transcendence of lack and a hedonistic interruption which introduces pleasure as discharge. It is the immanent process of desire which fills itself up, the continuum of intensities, the combination of fluxes, which replace both the law-authority and the pleasure-interruption. The process of desire is called 'joy', not lack or demand. Everything is permitted, except what would come and break up the integral process of desire, the assemblage. This is not something to do with Nature: on the contrary, it requires a great deal of artifice to exorcise the internal lack, the higher transcendent element and the apparent exterior. Ascesis, why not? Ascesis has always been the condition of desire, not its disciplining or prohibition. You will always find an ascesis if you think of desire. Now, it has been 'historically' necessary that a certain field of immanence should be possible at a particular moment, at a particular place. Chivalrous love properly speaking was not possible until the two fluxes had combined, the warrior flux and the erotic flux, in the sense that valour gave the right to love. But courtly love required a new demarcation in which valour became itself internal to love, and where love included the test.[13] One can say as much, in other conditions, of the masochist assemblage: the organization of humiliations and suffering in it appear less as a means of exorcizing anguish and so attaining a supposedly forbidden pleasure, than as a procedure, a particularly convoluted one, to constitute a body without organs and develop a continuous process of desire which pleasure, on the contrary, would come and interrupt.

We do not believe in general that sexuality has the role of an infrastructure in the assemblages of desire, nor that it constitutes an energy capable of transformation or of neutralization and sublimation. Sexuality can only be thought of as one flux among others, entering into conjunction with other fluxes, emitting particles which themselves enter into particular relationships of speed and slowness in the *vicinity* of certain other particles. No assemblage can be characterized by one flux exclusively. What a depressing idea of love, to make it a relation between two people, whose monotony must be vanquished as required by adding extra people. And it is not improved by the idea of leaving aside people altogether by bringing sexuality down to the construction of perverse or sadistic little machines which enclose sexuality in a theatre of phantasms: something dirty or stale is given off by all this, something which is too sentimental in any case, too narcissistic, as when a flux begins to revolve around itself and grow stale. So Félix's fine phrase 'desiring machines' ought to be given up for these reasons. The question about sexuality is: into the vicinity of what else does it enter to form such and such a hecceity, particular relations of movement and rest? The more it is articulated with other fluxes, the more it will remain sexuality, pure and simple sexuality, far from all idealizing sublimation. It will be all the more sexuality for itself, inventive, amazed, with neither phantasm which turns round and round nor idealization which leaps into the air: the masturbator is the only one who makes phantasms. Psychoanalysis is exactly a masturbation, a generalized, organized and coded narcissism. Sexuality does not allow itself to be sublimated, or phantasmed, because its concern is elsewhere, in the real vicinity of and in real combination with other fluxes, which exhaust or precipitate it – all depends on the moment and the assemblage. And it is not simply from one to the other of the two 'subjects' that this vicinity or combination takes place; it is in each of the two that several fluxes combine to form a bloc of becoming which makes demands on them both, music-becoming of Clara, woman- or child-becoming of Schumann. Not the man and woman as sexual entities, caught in a binary apparatus, but a molecular becoming, birth of a molecular woman in music, birth of molecular sonority in a woman. 'The relations between the two spouses profoundly change over the years, often without them realizing anything; while each change is a cause of suffering, even if it causes a certain joy . . . With each change a new being appears, a new rhythm is established . . . Sex is a changing thing, sometimes lively, sometimes resting, sometimes inflamed and sometimes dead.'[14] At each moment we are made up of lines which are variable at each instant, which may be combined in different ways, packets of lines, longitudes and latitudes, tropics and meridians, etc. There are no mono-fluxes. The analysis of the unconscious should be a geography rather than a history. Which lines appear blocked, moribund, closed in, dead-ended, falling into a black hole or exhausted, which others are active or lively, which allow something to escape and draw us along? Little Hans again: how was the line of the building and of the neighbours cut off from him; how was the Oedipal tree developed, what role did Professor Freud's branching-off play, why did the child seek refuge on the line of a horse-becoming, etc.? Psychoanalysis has always haunted parental and familial pathways, we should not reproach it for having chosen a particular way of branching off rather than another, but for having made a dead end out of this one, for having invented conditions of enunciation which crushed in advance the new utterances that it nevertheless gave rise to. We should get to the point of being able to say: your father, your mother, your grandmother, everything is fine, even the Name of the father, every entry is fine from the moment that there are multiple exits. But psychoanalysis has produced everything – except exits. 'Anywhere the rails lead us, anywhere at all, and if we come to an old offshoot rail line we don't know anything about, what the hell, we'll just take it, go down it, to see where it goes. And some year, by God, we'll boat down the Mississippi, always wanted to do that. Enough to last us a lifetime. And that's just how long I want to take to do it all.'[15]

II

The three misunderstandings of desire are relating it to: lack or law; a natural or spontaneous reality; pleasure or, above all, the festival. Desire is always assembled and fabricated, on a plane of immanence or of composition which must itself be constructed at the same time as desire assembles and fabricates. We do not simply mean that desire is historically determined. Historical determination involves a structural instance to play the role of law, or of cause, as a result of which desire is born. But desire is the real agent, merging each time with the variables of an assemblage. It is not lack or privation which leads to desire: one only feels lack in relation to an assemblage from which one is excluded, but one only desires as a result of an assemblage in which one is included (even if this were an association for banditry or revolt).

Machine, machinism, 'machinic': this does not mean either mechanical or organic. Mechanics is a system of closer and closer connections between dependent terms. The machine by contrast is a 'proximity' grouping between independent and heterogeneous terms (topological proximity is itself independent of distance or contiguity). What defines a machine assemblage is the shift of a centre of gravity along an abstract line. As in Kleist's marionette, it is this shift which gives rise to actual lines or movements. It may be said that the machine, in this sense, points to the unity of a machine operator. But this is wrong: the machine operator is present in the machine, 'in the centre of gravity', or rather of speed, which goes through him. That is why it is useless to say that certain movements are impossible for the machine – on the contrary, these are the movements such a machine makes because one of its parts is a man. Take the machine that has a dancer for one of its moving parts: one should not say that the machine cannot make some movement that only man is capable of making, but on the contrary that man is incapable of making this movement except as part of a certain machine. A gesture which comes from the East presupposes an Asiatic machine. The machine is a proximity grouping of man-tool-animal-thing. It is primary in relation to them since it is the abstract line which crosses them and makes them work together. It is always astride several structures, as in Tinguely's constructions. The machine, in requiring the heterogeneity of proximities, goes beyond the structures with their minimum conditions of homogeneity. A social machine always comes first in relation to the men and animals it takes into its 'stock'.

The history of technology shows that a tool is nothing without the variable machine assemblage which gives it a certain relationship of vicinity with man, animals and things: the hoplite weapons of the Greeks predate the hoplite assemblage but are used in a quite different way; the stirrup is a different tool depending on whether it is related to a nomadic war-machine, or whether, on the contrary, it has been taken up in the context of the feudal machine. It is the machine that makes the tool and not vice versa. An evolutionary line going from man to tool, and from tool to technological machine, is purely imaginary. The machine is social in its primary sense, and is primary in relation to the structures it crosses, to the men it makes use of, to the tools it selects, and to the technologies it promotes.

And it is similar with the organism: just as mechanics presupposes a social machine, the organism in turn supposes a *body without organs*, defined by its lines, axes and gradients, a whole, separate, machine functioning distinct from organic functions and from mechanical relationships. The intense egg, not at all maternal, but always contemporary with our organization, underlying our development. Abstract machines or bodies without organs – this is desire. There are many kinds, but they are definable by what occurs on them and in them: continuums of intensity, blocs of becoming, emissions of particles, combinations of fluxes.

Now it is these variables (which continuums? which becomings, which particles, which fluxes, which sorts of emission and combination?) which define 'regimes of signs'. It is not the regime which presupposes signs, it is the sign which presupposes a certain regime. It is, therefore, very doubtful whether the sign reveals a primacy of signifiance or of the signifier. It is rather the signifier which refers to a specific regime of signs, and probably not the most important or the most obvious. Semiology can only be a study of regimes, of their differences and their transformations. Sign refers to nothing in particular, except to regimes into which the variables of desire enter.

Let us take two examples out of the infinity of possible regimes. A centre can be thought of as an endogenous force, internal to the machine, which develops by circular irradiation in all directions, taking everything into its orbit, a mechanic continually jumping from one point to another, and from one circle to another. This then is a definition of a regime where the 'sign' keeps on referring back to the sign, in each circle and from one circle to the next, the totality of signs in turn referring back to a mobile signifier or to a centre of signifiance; and where interpretation, attribution of a signified, keeps on giving us back the signifier, as if to recharge the regime and overcome its entropy. There will be a group of intensities and fluxes which trace a particular 'map': at the centre the Despot, or the God, his temple or his house, his Face as an exposed face seen straight on, black hole on a white wall; the radiating organization of the circles, with a full bureaucracy to control the relations and movements from one circle to the next (the palace, the street, the village, the countryside, the scrub, the borders); the special role of the priest, who acts as interpreter or seer; the system's line of flight, which has to be barred, exorcized and stamped by a negative sign, patrolled by a kind of scapegoat, reverse image of the despot, whose role is regularly to take away everything that threatens or sullies the working of the machine. It can be seen that the line of gravity is, as it were, a mutation, and that the centre which traverses it, the 'mechanic', keeps jumping from one point to another: from the face of God to the faceless scapegoat via the scribes, the priests and the subjects. This is a regime that can be called signifying; but it depends on a specific regime of signs in so far as it expresses a state of fluxes and intensities.

Now take a different regime. We are no longer thinking of a simultaneous number of circles in infinite expansion, around a centre, such that each sign presupposes other signs, and the totality of signs a signifier. We are thinking of a little packet of signs, a little bloc of signs, which lines up along an endless straight line, marking on it a succession of processes, of fin-ished segments, each with a beginning and an end. This is a very different machine. Instead of an endogenous force which suffuses the whole, there is a decisive external event, a relation with the outside which is expressed as an emotion rather than as an Idea, an attempt or an action rather than an act of imagination. Instead of a centre of signifiance, there is a point of subjectivation which provides the starting-point of the line, and in relation to which a subject of enunciation is constituted, then a subject of utterance, even if this means that the utterance produces the enunciation again. A very different mechanism from that by which the signified provided another signifier: this time, it is the end of one process which marks the beginning of another, in linear succession. The linear segmentarity of succession is substituted for the circular segmentarity of simultaneity. The face has curiously changed the way it works: it is no longer the despotic face seen straight on; it is the authoritarian face, which turns away to put itself in profile. It is even a double turning-away, as Hölderlin said about Oedipus: the God, become Point of subjectivation, keeps on turning away from his subject, who also keeps turning away from his God. The faces line up, turn away and put themselves in profile. It is here that treason takes the place of trickery: the signifying regime was an economy of trickery, including the face of the despot, the operations of the scribe and the interpretations of the seer. But now the machination takes the form of a treason: it is by turning myself from God who turns from me, that I will accomplish the subjective mission of God, as the divine mission of my subjectivity. The prophet, the man of the double turning-away, has replaced the priest, interpreter or seer. The line of flight has completely changed its value: instead of being stamped by the negative sign which indicates the scapegoat, the line of flight has assumed the value of the positive sign; it merges with the gravity or velocity of the machine. But it is no less broken, segmentarized in a succession of finite processes which, at each occurrence, fall into a black hole. This, then, is another regime of signs, like another map-making: subjective regime or regime of passion, very different from the signifying regime.

   If we concentrate on these two for the moment, we wonder what they refer back to. Well, they refer back to anything, to periods and conditions that are very different. They can refer back to social formations, historical events, but also to pathological formations, psychological types, works of art, etc. Without there ever being any scope to reduce them in the slightest. For example, social formations: we can revive Robert Jaulin's terms, the Hebrew and the Pharaoh. It seems to us that the Pharaoh belongs to a highly signifying machine, and to a despotic regime which organizes intensities and fluxes in the irradiating circular style that we have tried to define. The Hebrew, in contrast, has lost the Temple, he throws himself into a line of flight to which he attributes the greatest positive value; but he segmentarizes this line in a series of finite authoritarian 'processes'. It is the Ark which is now just a little packet of signs shooting out along a desert-line, between the land and the waters, instead of being the Temple, central, immobile and omnipresent in the harmony of the elements. It is the scapegoat who becomes the most intense figure – we will be the goat and the lamb, God become slaughtered animal: 'Let evil come back upon us' – Moses invokes the process or *demand* – too oppressive to bear – which must be redirected and distributed into successive segments, contract-process that is always precarious. The double, linear turning-away is imposed as the new figure which connects God and his prophet (Jerome Lindon has demonstrated this in the case of Jonah; it is also what the sign of Cain is; it is also what the sign of Christ is to be). The Passion, subjectivation.

Then we think of something quite different, in a totally different sphere: how, in the nineteenth century, there becomes apparent a distinction between two major kinds of delirium. On the one hand, paranoid and interpretative delirium, whose starting-point is an endogenous force like a centre of signifiance, which radiates out in all directions, constantly referring one sign back to another, and the totality of the signs to a central signifier (despot, phallus, castration, with all the leaps, all the mutations from the castrating Master to the castrated goat). On the other hand, a very different form of delirium, called monomaniac, or passionate and concerned with demand: an external occurrence, a point of subjectivation, which can be anything, a little local packet of signs, an arc, a blink, a fetish, lingerie, a shoe, a face that turns away – this point of subjectivation is swallowed up along a straight line which will be segmentarized in successive processes with variable intervals. Delirium of action rather than idea, say psychiatrists; of emotion rather than imagination; dependent on a 'postulate' or a concise formula rather than a germ of development. We have seen how psychiatry, at its beginning, found itself trapped between these two kinds of delirium: this was not a matter of symptomatology, but a whole new body of material arrived from both sides or was found to be available at that moment, overflowing the system of what was, until then, called 'madness'. A person suffering from a passionate or subjective delirium starts a process, indicated by a point of subjectivation: 'He loves me', 'he' gave me a sign; I constitute myself as a subject of enunciation (flux of pride, high intensity); I fall back to the condition of subject of utterances ('He is cheating me', 'He's a traitor', low intensity). And then a second 'process' begins, as the passionate person lodges himself in the line of flight which goes from black hole to black hole. Tristan and Isolde follow the line of passion of the boat which takes them away: Tristan, Isolde, Isolde, Tristan . . . There is here a type of redundancy, passionate or subjective, *the redundancy of resonance, very different from the redundancy of signifying or of frequency.*

Our distinctions are undoubtedly too hasty. We ought to take each specific case and search in it for its specific machine, or 'body without organs'; and then find out what happens, particles or fluxes, what regime of signs. If the machine is not a mechanism, and if the body is not an organism, it is always then that desire assembles. But it is not in the same way as a masochist assembles, or a drug addict, or an alcoholic, or an anorexic, etc. Homage to Fanny: the case of anorexia. It is a question of food fluxes, but combined with other fluxes, clothes fluxes, for example (specifically anorexic elegance,

Fanny's trinity: Virginia Woolf, Murnau, Kay Kendall). The anorexic consists of a body without organs with voids and fullnesses. The alternation of stuffing and emptying: anorexic feasts, the imbibings of fizzy drinks. We should not even talk about alternation: void and fullness are like two demarcations of intensity; the point is always to float in one's own body. It is not a matter of a refusal of the body, it is a matter of a refusal of the organism, of a refusal of what the organism makes the body undergo. Not regression at all, but involution, involuted body. The anorexic void has nothing to do with a lack, it is on the contrary a way of escaping the organic constraint of lack and hunger at the mechanical mealtime. There is a whole plane of construction of the anorexic, making oneself an anorganic body (which does not mean asexual: on the contrary, woman-becoming of every anorexic). Anorexia is a political system, a micro-politics: to escape from the norms of consumption in order not to be an object of consumption oneself. It is a feminine protest, from a woman who wants to have a functioning of the body and not simply organic and social functions which make her dependent. She will turn consumption against itself: she will often be a model – she will often be a cook, a peripatetic cook, who will make something for others to eat, or else she will like being at the table either without eating, or else multiplying the absorption of little things, of little substances. Cook-model, a mixture that can only exist in this assemblage, this system, and which will be dissolved in different ones. Her goal is to wrest particles from food, minute particles with which she will be able to create her void as well as her fullness, depending on whether she gives them out or receives them. Anorexics are enthusiasts: they live treason or the double turning-away in several ways. They betray hunger, because hunger tricks them by making them subject to the organism; they betray the family because the family betrays them by subjecting them to the family meal and a whole family politics of consumption (to put in its place an uninterrupted consumption, but one that is neutralized,

sanitized); finally they betray food, because food is treacherous by nature (the anorexic thinks that food is full of
grubs and poisons, worms and bacteria, fundamentally bad,
hence the need to select and extract particles from it, or to spit
it back out). 'I'm starving,' she says, grabbing two 'slimming
yoghurts'. Trick-the-hunger, trick-the-family, trick-the-food.
In short, anorexia is a history of politics: to be the involuted of
the organism, the family or the consumer society. There is
politics as soon as there is a continuum of intensities (anorexic
void and fullness), emission and conquest of food particles
(constitution of a body without organs, in opposition to a
dietary or organic regime), and above all combination of
fluxes (the food flux enters into relation with a clothes flux, a
flux of language, a flux of sexuality: a whole, molecular
woman-becoming in the anorexic, whether man or woman). It
is what we call a regime of signs. Above all, it is not a matter of
partial objects. It is true that psychiatry and psychoanalysis
do not understand, because they bring everything down to the
level of a neuro-organic or symbolic code ('lack, lack . . .'). So
the second question arises: why does the anorexic assemblage
come so close to going off the rails, to becoming lethal? What
are the dangers it constantly skirts and the dangers into which
it falls? This is a question that must be taken up by a method
other than psychoanalysis: we must try to find out what
dangers arise *in the middle of* a real experiment, and not the lack
dominating a pre-established interpretation. People are
always in the middle of some business, where nothing may be
designated as its origin. Always things encountering each
other, never things diminishing each other's contribution. A
cartography and never a symbolics.

We thought that this digression on anorexia should make
things clearer. Perhaps, on the other hand, we should not
multiply examples, because there are an infinite number of
them pointing in different directions. Anorexia will assume
increasing importance as a result. In the first place, we should
distinguish in a regime of signs *the abstract machine which defines*

it, and the actual assemblages into which it enters: thus the machine of subjectivation, and the assemblages which realize it, in the history of the Hebrews; but equally in the course of passionate delirium, in the construction of a work, etc. Between these assemblages, which operate in very different circumstances, and at very different periods, there will be no causal dependence, but mutual branchings, 'proximities' independent of distance or of spatio-temporal proximity. The same plane will be taken up and taken up again at very different levels, depending on whether things happen on 'my' body, on a social body, a geographical body (but my body is also a geography, or a people, or peoples). Not that each person reproduces a fragment of universal history; but we are always in a zone of intensity or flux, which is common to our enterprise, to a very remote global enterprise, to very distant geographical environments. Hence a secret of delirium: it haunts certain regions of history which are not arbitrarily chosen; delirium is not personal or a family matter, it is world-historical ('I am a beast, a Negro . . . I dreamt of crusades, expeditions of discovery that are completely foreign to us, republics without histories, stifled religious wars, revolution of customs, shifts of races and of continents'). And areas of history haunt deliriums and works, without it being possible to establish causal or symbolic connections. There may be a desert of the hypochondriac body, a steppe of the anorexic body, a capital of the paranoid body: these are not metaphors between societies and organisms, but collectives without organs which are realized in a people, a society, a set of surroundings or an 'ego'. The same abstract machine in very different assemblages. History is constantly being remade, but conversely it is constantly being made by each of us, on his own body. Which famous person would you like to have been, at what period would you like to have lived? And if you were a plant, or a landscape? But you are all this already, your mistake is simply in the answers. You are always an assemblage for an abstract machine, which is realized

elsewhere in other assemblages. You are always in the middle
of something; plant, animal or landscape. We know our rela-
tives and associates, never our neighbours who might be from
another planet, who always are from another planet. Only
neighbours matter. History is an introduction to delirium, but
reciprocally delirium is the only introduction to history.

In the second place, there are an infinite number of regimes
of signs. We have looked at two, very limited ones: a
Signifying Regime, which is said to be realized in an imperial
despotic assemblage, and also, under other conditions, in an
interpretative paranoid assemblage; a Subjective Regime,
which is said to be realized in a contractual authoritarian
assemblage, and also in a passionate [*passionnel*] or demanding
monomaniac assemblage. But there are so many others, both
at the level of abstract machines and of their assemblages.
Anorexia itself sketched out another regime which we reduced
to this schema only for convenience. The regimes of signs are
innumerable: multiple semiotics of 'primitive peoples', semiotics of nomads (and those of the desert are not the same as
those of the steppe; and the journey of the Hebrews is something different again), the semiotics of sedentary peoples (and
how many combinations of the sedentary, and of sedentary-
nomad, there are). Significance and the signifier enjoy no
privilege. We should simultaneously study all the regimes of
pure signs, from the point of view of the abstract machines
they put into play, and also all the concrete assemblages, from
the point of view of the mixtures they carry out. A concrete
semiotics is a mix, a mixture of several regimes of signs. Every
concrete semiotics is of the little Negro or of the Javanese type.
The Hebrews straddle a nomadic semiotics, which they profoundly transform, and an imperial semiotics, which they
dream of restoring on new foundations by reconstructing the
Temple. There is no pure condition of passion in delirium, a
paranoiac element is always combined with it (Clérambault,
the psychiatrist who distinguished most clearly between the
two types of delirium, underlined at the same time their mixed

nature). If we consider a detail, like the face-function in semiotics of painting, we see clearly how the mixtures are created: Jean Paris showed that the Byzantine imperial face, seen straight on, left depth outside the picture, between the picture and the viewer; whilst the quattrocento integrated depth by providing the face with a degree of profile or even of turning away; but a picture like Duccio's *Appeal to Tiberius* creates a mix whereby one of the disciples still exemplifies the Byzantine face while the other enters into a specifically passionate [*passionnel*] relation with the Christ figure.[16] What can be said about huge assemblages like 'capitalism' or 'socialism'? The economy of each one and its financing put into play very varied types of regimes of signs and abstract machines. For its part, psychoanalysis is incapable of analysing regimes of signs because it is itself a mix which operates simultaneously by signifiance and subjectivation, without noticing the composite nature of its approach (its operations proceed through infinite despotic signifiance, while its organizations are passionate [*passionnel*], initiating an unlimited series of linear processes where at each instance the psychoanalyst – whether the same or a new one – plays the role of 'point of subjectivation', with the turning-away of faces: psychoanalysis is doubly interminable). A general semiotic regime should therefore have a first component which is *generative*; but it would simply be a matter of showing how an actual assemblage brings into play several regimes of pure signs or several abstract machines, putting them into play in one another's mechanisms. A second component would be *transformational*; but now it would be a question of showing how one pure regime of signs can be translated into another, with what transformations, what unassimilable residues, what variations and innovations. This second point of view would be more profound, since it would show, not now simply how semiotics mix, but how new semiotics are detached and produced, and how abstract machines are themselves capable of mutations, inspiring new assemblages.

In the third place, a regime of signs is never to be confused with either language or a language-system. One can still determine abstract organic functions which presuppose language (information, expression, signification, enactment, etc.). One can even, in the manner of Saussure and even more of Chomsky, think of an abstract machine which presupposes no knowledge of a language: homogeneity and invariance are postulated, whether the invariants are conceived as structural or 'genetic' (hereditary programming). Such a machine can integrate specifically syntactic or even semantic regimes; it will push aside the very varied variables and assemblages which influence a single language into a sort of depository labelled 'pragmatics'. We will not fault such a machine for being abstract, but on the contrary, for not being abstract enough. For it is not the organic functions of language, nor an 'organon' of a language-system, that determine the regimes of signs. On the contrary, it is the regimes of signs (pragmatics) that fix the collective assemblages of enunciation in a language as flux of expression, at the same time as the machine assemblages of desire are fixed in fluxes of content. So that a language-system is as much a heterogeneous flux in itself as in a relationship of reciprocal presupposition with fluxes that are heterogeneous both in regard to each other and to the language-system. An abstract machine is never a thing of language, but shapes very varied combinations, emissions and continuations of fluxes.

There are no functions of language or of the organ or corpus of a language-system but rather machinic functionings with collective assemblages. Literature, '*business of the people*'; why can the most solitary person, Kafka, say this? Pragmatics is called to take upon itself the whole of linguistics. What does Roland Barthes do, in his own evolution in regard to semiotics? – he begins with a notion of the 'signifier', to become more and more 'passionate' [*passionnel*], then seems to elaborate a regime that is both open and secret, all the more collective for being his particular one: behind an apparently personal lexical regime, a syntactic network flourishes, and behind this network a pragmatics of particles and fluxes, like a cartography which is reversible, capable of modification and colouring-in, in all sorts of ways. Making a book which would have to be mentally coloured-in is perhaps what Barthes found in Loyola; linguistic ascesis. He appears to 'explain himself'; in reality he is creating a pragmatics of language. Félix Guattari has written a text on the following linguistic principles, which take up in their own way some theses of Weinreich and above all of Labov: (1) it is pragmatics which is essential because it is the true politics, the micro-politics of language; (2) there are no universals or invariants of language, no 'competence' separate from 'performances'; (3) there is no abstract machine internal to language, only abstract machines which provide a language with a particular collective assemblage of enunciation (there is no 'subject' of enunciation), at the same time as they provide content with a particular machine assemblage of desire (there is no signifier of desire); (4) there are therefore several languages in a language, at the same time as there are all sorts of fluxes in the contents that are sent out, combined and continued. The point is not 'bilingual', 'multilingual'; the point is that every language is itself so bilingual, itself so multilingual, that one can stutter in one's own language, be a foreigner in one's own language, that is push ever further the points of de-territorialization of assemblages. A language is criss-crossed by lines of flight that carry off its vocabulary and syntax. And abundance of vocabulary and richness of syntax are only means to serve a line whose test of quality is by contrast its restraint, its conciseness, even its abstraction: an unstressed involuting line that determines the meanders of a phrase or a text; that inflects every redundancy and bursts figures of style. It is the pragmatic line, of gravity or velocity, whose ideal poverty masters the richness of the others.

There are no functions of language, only regimes of signs which simultaneously combine fluxes of expression and fluxes of content, determining assemblages of desire in the latter, and assemblages of enunciation in the former, each caught up in the other. Language is never the only flux of expression; and a flux of expression is never on its own, but always related to fluxes of content determined by the regime of signs. When we consider language on its own, we are not making a true abstraction; on the contrary, we are depriving ourselves of the conditions which would make possible the attribution of an abstract machine. When we consider a flux of writing on its own, it can only turn circles round itself, falling into a black hole where the only sound for ever after is the echo of the question. 'What is writing? What is writing?', without anything ever coming out. What Labov discovers in language to be immanent variation, irreducible either to the structure or the development, seems to us to go back to states of combination of fluxes, in content and expression.[17] When a word assumes a different meaning, or even enters into a different syntax, we can be sure that it has crossed another flux or that it has been introduced to a different regime of signs (for instance, the sexual sense that a word from elsewhere can assume, and vice versa). It is never a matter of metaphor; there are no metaphors, only combinations. The poetry of François Villon: combination of words with three fluxes, theft, homosexuality, gambling.[18] The extraordinary attempt of Louis Wolfson, 'the young schizophrenic student of languages', is difficult to reduce to normal psychoanalytic and linguistic considerations: the way he translates his mother tongue *at top speed* into a mixture of other languages – this way, not of leaving his mother tongue, since he retains its sense and sound, but of putting it to flight and deterritorializing it – is intimately connected to the anorexic flux of food, to the way he snatches particles from this flux, combines them at top speed and combines them with verbal particles snatched from his mother tongue.[19] Emitting verbal particles which enter the 'proximity' of food particles, etc.

What would identify a pragmatics of language, in relation

to its syntactic and semantic aspects, would therefore not be its relation to the determinations of psychology or of situation, circumstances or intentions, but rather the fact that it reaches the extreme of abstraction in the context of machine components. It would seem that regimes of signs refer simultaneously to two systems of co-ordinates. Either the assemblages that they determine are reduced to a principal component as organization of power, in a stable order with dominant meanings (thus despotic signifiance, the passionate [*passionnel*] subject of enunciation, etc.); or else they will be caught in the movement which combines their lines of flight even further, making them discover new connotations or directions, constantly excavating a different language within the first one. Either the abstract machine will be overcoding – it will overcode every assemblage with a signifier, with a subject, etc. – or else it will be mutant, mutational, and will discover behind every assemblage the point that undoes the basic organization, making the assemblage shoot off into a different one. Either everything is related to a *plane of organization and development* which is structural or genetic, form or subject; or everything is launched on a *plane of consistence* which only knows differential speeds and hecceities. According to one regime of co-ordinates, it may still be said that the American language today contaminates all languages, imperialism: but according to the other system of reference, it is Anglo-American which finds itself contaminated by the most diverse regimes, Black English, Yellow, Red or White English, and which is everywhere in flight, New York, city without language. To take account of these alternatives, we must introduce a third component which is no longer simply generative or transformational, but *diagrammatic or pragmatic*. We must discover in every regime and every assemblage the specific value of the existing lines of flight: how here they are stamped with a negative sign; how over there they gain a positive quality, but are cut up and bartered in successive processes; how elsewhere they fall into black holes; how elsewhere again they enter the service of a war-machine; or else bring a work of art to life. And as they are all this at once, they make at each moment a diagram, a map of what is blocked, overcoded, or, on the contrary, mutating, on the route to liberation, in the process of outlining a particular fragment for a plane of consistence. Diagrammatism consists in pushing a language to the plane where 'immanent' variation no longer depends on a structure or development, but on the combination of mutating fluxes, on their productions of speed, on their combinations of particles (to the point where food particles, sexual particles, verbal particles, etc., reach their zone of proximity or indiscernibility: abstract machine).

Note by G. D.

I think this is what I wanted to do when I worked on some writers, Sacher-Masoch, Proust or Lewis Carroll. What interested me, or should have interested me, was not the psychoanalysis, or the psychiatry, or the linguistics, but the regimes of signs of a given author. This only became clear to us when Félix arrived, and we did a book on Kafka. My ideal, when I write about an author, would be to write nothing that could cause him sadness, or if he is dead, that might make him weep in his grave. Think of the author you are writing about. Think of him so hard that he can no longer be an object, and equally so that you cannot identify with him. Avoid the double shame of the scholar and the familiar. Give back to an author a little of the joy, the energy, the life of love and politics that he knew how to give and invent. So many dead writers must have wept over what has been written about them. I hope that Kafka was pleased with the book that we did on him, and it is for that reason that the book pleased nobody.

Criticism and *the clinic* ought strictly to be identical: but criticism would be, as it were, the outline of the plane of consistence of a work, a sieve which would extract the particles emitted or picked up, the fluxes combined, the becomings in play; the clinic, in accordance with its precise meaning, would be the outline of lines on this plane or the way in which the lines outline the plane, which of them are dead-ended or blocked, which cross voids, which continue, and most importantly the line of steepest gradient, how it draws in the rest, towards what destination. A clinic without psychoanalysis or interpretation, a criticism without linguistics or signifiance. Criticism, art of combinations [*conjugaisons*] like the clinic, art of declension. It would simply be a matter of knowing three things.

(1) The function of the proper name (the proper name, here, is precisely not a reference to a particular person as author or subject of enunciation; it refers to one or several assemblages; the proper name brings about an individuation by 'hecceity', not at all by subjectivity). Charlotte Brontë designates a state of the winds more than a person; Virginia Woolf designates a state of reigns, ages and sexes. An assemblage may have been in existence for a long time before it receives its proper name which gives it a special consistence as if it were thus separated from a more general regime to assume a kind of autonomy: as in 'sadism', 'masochism'. Why, at a certain moment, does the proper name isolate an assemblage, why does it make it into a particular regime of signs, according to a transformational component? Why is there not also 'Nietzscheism', 'Proustism', 'Kafkaism', 'Spinozism', on the lines of a generalized clinic, that is, a semiology of regimes of signs which is anti-psychiatric, anti-psychoanalytic, anti-philosophical? And what will an isolated, named regime of signs become in the clinical current which carries it away? What is fascinating in medicine is that the proper name of a doctor can be used to designate a group of symptoms: Parkinson, Roger . . . It is here that the proper name becomes proper name and finds its function. What has happened is that the doctor has created a new grouping, a new individuation of symptoms, a new hecceity, has broken up regimes which have up to this point been mixed together, has reunited sequences of regimes which up to this point were separate.[20] But what distinction is there between the doctor and the sick man? It is the sick

man too who gives his proper name. This is Nietzsche's idea: the writer and the artist as doctor-sick man of a civilization. The more you create your own regime of signs, the less you will be a person or a subject, the more you will be a 'collective' that meets other collectives, that combines and interconnects with others, reactivating, inventing, bringing to the future, bringing about non-personal individuations.

(2) A regime of signs is no more determined by linguistics than by psychoanalysis. On the contrary, it is the regime of signs itself that will determine a particular assemblage of enunciation in the fluxes of expression and a particular assemblage of desire in the fluxes of content. And by content we do not just mean what a writer talks about, his 'subjects', in the double sense of the themes he deals with and the characters he puts before us, but much more the states of desire internal and external to the work, and which are composed along with it, in 'proximity'. Never consider a flux all on its own; the content–expression distinction is so relative that a flux of content may even come into the expression, in so far as it enters into an assemblage of enunciation in relation to other fluxes. Every assemblage is collective, since it is made up of several fluxes which carry along the characters and things, and which are only to be divided or reassembled as multiplicities. For example, in Sacher- Masoch the flux of pain and humiliation is expressed as a contractual assemblage, the contracts of Masoch, but these contracts are also contents in relation to the expression of the authoritarian or despotic woman. We have to ask, each time, what the flux of writing is connected with. Thus the love-letter as assemblage of enunciation: a love-letter is most important; we tried to describe and demonstrate how it worked, and in connection with what, in the case of Kafka – the first task would be to study the regimes of signs employed by an author, and what mixtures he uses (*generative component*). Staying with the two representative examples that we have picked out, the despotic signifying regime and the subjective passionate [*passionnel*] regime, we can see how they are combined in Kafka – the Castle as irradiating despotic centre, but also as succession of finite Pro-

cesses in a series of contiguous parts. And see how differently they are combined in Proust: in relation to Charlus, core of a galaxy whose spirals include utterances and contents; in relation to Albertine, who passes in contrast through a series of finite linear processes, processes of sleep, processes of jealousy, processes of imprisonment. Few authors have been able to match Proust in bringing into play a multitude of regimes of signs out of which to compose their work. In addition, each time new regimes are produced, where what was expression in the earlier ones becomes content in relation to new forms of expression; a new usage of the language-system excavates a new language-system in language (*transformational component*).

(3) But the essential point, in the end, is the way in which all these regimes of signs move along a line of gradient, variable with each author, tracing out a plane of consistence or composition which characterizes a given work or group of works: not a plane in the mind, but an immanent real plane, which was not pre-existent, and which blends all the lines, the intersection of all the regimes (*diagrammatic   component*): Virginia Woolf's Wave, Lovecraft's Hypersphere, Proust's Spider's Web, Kleist's Programme, Kafka's K-function, the Rhizosphere . . . it is here that there is no longer any fixed distinction between content and expression. We no longer know if it is a flux of words or of alcohol, we are so drunk on pure water, but equally because we are talking so much with 'materials which are more immediate, more fluid, more burning than words'. We no longer know if it is a flux of food or of words, so much is anorexia a regime of signs, and the signs a regime of calories[21]* (the verbal aggression when someone breaks the silence too early in the morning; Nietzsche's dietary regime and that of Proust and Kafka, are also forms of writing, and they understand it as such; eating- speaking, writing-loving, you will never catch a flux all on its own). No longer are elements on one side and syntagms on the other; there are only *particles* entering into each other's proximity, on the basis of a plane of immanence. 'I had the idea', says Virginia Woolf, 'that what I wanted to do now was to saturate each atom.' And here again there are no

longer any forms being organized as a result of a structure, or being developed as a result of a genesis; nor are there any subjects, persons or characters, which let themselves be attributed, formed or developed. There are only particles left, particles definable solely by relationships of movement and rest, speed and slowness, constructions of differential speeds (and it is not necessarily speed that wins; it is not necessarily slowness that is the last to get there). There are now only hecceities left, individuations which are precise and without subject, which are definable solely by affects or powers (and it is not necessarily the strongest that wins; it is not the one who is the richest in affects). For us, what is important in Kafka is precisely the way in which, throughout the regimes of signs, he uses or anticipates (capitalism, bureaucracy, fascism, Stalinism, all the 'satanic powers of the future'), he puts them in flight or movement on a plane of consistence that is like the immanent field of desire, always incomplete, but never lacking, or legislating, or subjectivating. Literature? But here we have Kafka putting literature into an immediate relationship with a minority-machine, a new collective assemblage of enunciation for German (an assemblage of minorities in the Austrian Empire had already been Masoch's idea, in a different way). See how Kleist put literature into an immediate relationship with a war-machine. In short, the criticism-clinic should follow the line of steepest gradient in a work, at the same time as reaching its plane of consistence. Nathalie Sarraute made a highly important distinction when she opposed to the organization of forms and the development of persons and characters this quite different plane traversed by particles of an unknown material, 'which, like droplets of mercury, constantly tend to join up and intermingle in a common mass through the envelopes which separate them':[22] collective assemblage of enunciation, deterritorialized ritornello, plane of consistence of desire, where the proper name reaches its highest individuality by losing all personality – imperceptible-becoming, *Josephine the chick.*

4

Many Politics

I

Whether we are individuals or groups, we are made up of lines and these lines are very varied in nature. The first kind of line which forms us is segmentary – of rigid segmentarity (or rather there are already many lines of this sort): family – profession; job – holiday; family – and then school – and then the army – and then the factory – and then retirement. And each time, from one segment to the next, they speak to us, saying: 'Now you're not a baby any more'; and at school, 'You're not at home now'; and in the army, 'You're not at school now' . . . In short, all kinds of clearly defined segments, in all kinds of directions, which cut us up in all senses, packets of segmentarized lines. At the same time, we have lines of segmentarity which are much more supple, as it were molecular. It's not that they are more intimate or personal – they run through societies and groups as much as individuals. They trace out little modifications, they make detours, they sketch out rises and falls: but they are no less precise for all this, they even direct irreversible processes. But rather than molar lines with segments, they are molecular fluxes with thresholds or quanta. *A threshold is crossed, which does not necessarily coincide with a segment of more visible lines.* Many things happen on this second kind of line – becomings, micro-becomings, which don't even have the same rhythm as our 'history'. This is why family histories, registrations, commemorations, are so unpleasant, whilst our true changes take place elsewhere – another politics, another time, another individuation. A profession is a rigid segment, but also what happens beneath it, the connections, the attractions and repulsions, which do not coincide with the segments, the forms of madness which are secret but which nevertheless relate to the public authorities: for example, being a teacher, or a judge, a barrister, an accountant, a cleaning lady? At the same time, again, there is a third kind of line, which is even more strange: as if something carried us away, across our segments, but also across our thresholds, towards a destination which is unknown, not foreseeable, not pre-existent. This line is simple, abstract, and yet is the most complex of all, the most tortuous: it is the line of gravity or velocity, the line of flight and of the greatest gradient ('the line that the centre of gravity must describe is certainly very simple, and, so he believed, straight in the majority of cases . . . but, from another point of view, this line has something exceedingly mysterious, for, according to him, it is nothing other than the progression of the soul of the dancer. . . .'[1]) This line appears to arise [*surgir*] afterwards, to become detached from the two others, if indeed it succeeds in detaching itself. For perhaps there are people who do not have this line, who have only the two others, or who have only one, who live on only one. Nevertheless, in another sense, this line has always been there, although it is the opposite of a destiny: it does not have to detach itself from the others, rather it is the first, the others are derived from it. In any case, the three lines are immanent, caught up in one another. We have as many tangled lines as a hand. We are complicated in a different way from a hand. What we call by different names – schizoanalysis, micro-politics, pragmatics, diagrammatism, rhizomatics, cartography – has no other object than the study of these lines, in groups or as individuals.

Fitzgerald explains, in a wonderful short story, that a life always goes at several rhythms, at several speeds.[2] Though Fitzgerald is a living drama – defining life as a demolition process – his text is sombre, but no less exemplary for that, each sentence inspiring love. His genius is never so great as when he speaks of his loss of genius. Thus, he says that for him there were at first great segments – rich–poor, young–old, success–loss of success, health–sickness, love–love's drying up, creativity–sterility – which were related to social events (economic crisis, stock market crash, rise of the cinema which replaced the novel, formation of fascism, all sorts of things which could be said to be heterogeneous, but whose segments respond to and precipitate each other). Fitzgerald calls these 'cuts' [*coupures*]; each segment marks or can mark a cut. This is a type of line, the segmented line, which concerns us all at a particular time, at a particular place. Whether it heads towards degradation or success does not alter much (on this model a successful life is not the best, the American Dream is as much in the street-sweeper starting out to become a multimillionaire as in the multimillionaire himself, the opposite; the same segments). And Fitzgerald says something else, at the same time: there are lines of crack [*fêlure*], which do not coincide with the lines of great segmentary cuts. This time we might say that a plate cracks. But it is rather when everything is going well, or everything goes better on the other line, that the crack happens on this new line – secret, imperceptible, marking a threshold of lowered resistance, or the rise of a threshold of exigency: you can no longer stand what you put up with before, even yesterday; the distribution of desires has changed in us, our relationships of speed and slowness have been modified, a new type of anxiety comes upon us, but also a new serenity. Fluxes have moved, it is when your health is at its best, your riches most assured, your talent most manifest, that the little cracking which will move the line obliquely starts to happen. Or the opposite: things go better for you when everything cracks on the other line, producing immense relief. Not being able to bear something any longer can be a progression, but it can also be an old man's fear, or the development of a paranoia. It can be a political or affective appraisal which is perfectly correct. We do not change, we do not age, in the same way – from one line to the other. Nevertheless, the supple line is not more personal, more intimate. Micro-cracks are also collective, no less than macro-cuts are personal. And then, Fitzgerald speaks of yet another line, a third, which he calls *rupture*. It might be thought that nothing has changed, and nevertheless everything has changed. Certainly it is not the great segments, changes or even journeys which produce this line; but neither is it the most secret mutations, the mobile and fluent thresholds, although these approximate more closely to it. It might be said rather that an 'absolute' threshold has been reached. There are no longer secrets. You have become like everyone, but in fact you have turned the 'everyone' into a *becoming*. You have become imperceptible, clandestine. You have undergone a curious stationary journey. Despite the different tones, it is a little like the way in which Kierkegaard describes the knight of the faith, ONLY MOVEMENTS CONCERN ME:[3] the knight no longer has segments of resignation, but neither does he have the suppleness of a poet or of a dancer, he does not make himself obvious, he resembles rather a bourgeois, a tax-collector, a tradesman, he dances with so much precision that they say that he is only walking or even staying still, he blends into the wall but the wall has become alive, he is painted grey on grey, or like the Pink Panther he has painted the world in his own colour, he has acquired something invulnerable, and he knows that by loving, even by loving and for loving, one must be self-contained, abandon love and the ego . . . (it is curious that Lawrence has written similar passages). There is now only an abstract line, a pure movement which is difficult to discover, he never begins, he takes things by the middle, he is always in the middle – in the middle of two other lines? 'Only movements concern me.'

A cartography is suggested today by Deligny when he follows the course of autistic children: the lines of custom, and also the supple lines where the child produces a loop, finds something, claps his hands, hums a ritornello, retraces his steps, and then the 'lines of wandering' mixed up in the two others.[4] All these lines are tangled. Deligny produces a geo-analysis, an analysis of lines which takes his path far from psychoanalysis, and which relates not only to autistic children, but to all children, to all adults (watch someone walking down the street and see what little inventions he introduces into it, if he is not too caught up in his rigid segmentarity, what little inventions he puts there), and not only their walk, but their gestures, their affects, their language, their style. First of all, we should give a more precise status to the three lines. For the molar lines of rigid segmentarity, we can indicate a certain number of charac-teristics which explain their assemblage, or rather their functioning in the assemblages of which they form part (and there is no assemblage which does not include them). Here therefore are the approximate characteristics of the first kind of line.

(1) Segments depend on binary machines which can be very varied if need be. Binary machines of social classes; of sexes, man–woman; of ages, child–adult; of races, black–white; of sectors, public–private; of subjectivations, ours–not ours. These binary machines are all the more com-plex for cutting across each other, or colliding against each other, confronting each other, and they cut us up in all sorts of directions. And they are not roughly dualistic, they are rather dichotomic: they can operate diachronically (if you are neither *a* nor *b*, then you are *c*: dualism has shifted, and no longer relates to simultaneous elements to choose between, but suc-cessive choices; if you are neither black nor white, you are a half-breed; if you are neither man nor woman, you are a transvestite: each time the machine with binary elements will produce binary choices between elements which are not pre-sent at the first cutting-up).

(2) Segments also imply devices of power, which vary greatly among themselves, each fixing the code and the territory of the corresponding segment. These are the devices

which have been analysed so profoundly by Foucault, who refused to see in them the simple emanations of a pre-existing State apparatus. Each device of power is a code-territory complex (do not approach my territory, it is I who give the orders here . . .). M. de Charlus collapses at Mme Verdurin's, because he has ventured beyond his own territory and his code no longer works. The segmentarity of adjacent offices in Kafka. It is by discovering this segmentarity and this heterogeneity of modern powers that Foucault was able to break with the hollow abstractions of the State and of 'the' law and renew all the assumptions of political analysis. It is not that the apparatus of the State has no meaning: it has itself a very special function, in as much as it overcodes all the segments, both those that it takes on itself at a given moment and those that it leaves outside itself. Or rather the apparatus of the State is a concrete assemblage which realizes the machine of overcoding of a society. This machine in its turn is thus not the State itself, it is the abstract machine which organizes the dominant utterances and the established order of a society, the dominant languages and knowledge, conformist actions and feelings, the segments which prevail over others. The abstract machine of overcoding ensures the homogenization of different segments, their convertibility, their translatability, it regulates the passages from one side to the other, and the prevailing force under which this takes place. It does not depend on the State, but its effectiveness depends on the State as the assemblage which realizes it in a social field (for example, different monetary segments, different kinds of money have rules of convertibility, between themselves and with goods, which refer to a central bank as State apparatus). Greek geometry functioned as an abstract machine which organized the social space, in the conditions of the concrete assemblage of power of the city. We should ask today which are the abstract machines of overcoding, which are exercised as a result of the forms of the modern State. One can even conceive of 'forms of knowledge' which make their offers of service to the State, proposing themselves for its realization, claiming to provide the best machines for the tasks or the aims of the State: today informatics? But also the human sciences? There are no sciences of the State but there are abstract machines which have relationships of interdependence with the State. This is why, on the line of rigid segmentarity, one must distinguish the *devices of power* which code the diverse segments, the *abstract machine* which overcodes them and regulates their relationships and the *apparatus of the State* which realizes this machine.

(3) Finally, all rigid segmentarity, all the lines of rigid segmentarity, enclose a certain plane, which concerns both forms and their development, subjects and their formation. *A plane of organization* which always has at its disposal a supplementary dimension (overcoding). The education of the subject and the harmonization of the form have constantly haunted our culture, inspired the segmentations, the planifications, the binary machines which cut them and the abstract machines which cut them again. As Pierre Fleutiaux says, when an outline begins to tremble, when a segment wavers, we call the terrible Lunette to cut things up, the laser which puts forms in order and subjects in their place.[5]

The status of the other type of lines seems to be completely different. The segments here are not the same, proceeding by thresholds, constituting becomings, blocs of becoming, marking continuums of intensity, combinations of fluxes. The abstract machines here are not the same, they are mutating and not overcoding, marking their mutations at each threshold and each combination. The plane is not the same, *plane of consistence or of immanence* which tears from forms particles between which there are now only relationships of speed and slowness, and tears from subjects affects which now only carry out individuations by 'hecceity'. The binary machines no longer engage with this real, not because the dominant segment would change (a particular class, a particular sex . . .), nor because mixtures like bisexuality or class-mixing would be imposed: on the contrary, because the molecular lines make fluxes of deterritorialization shoot between the segments, fluxes which no longer belong to one or to the other, but which constitute an asymmetrical becoming of the two, molecular sexuality which is no longer that of a man or of a woman, molecular masses which no longer have the outline of a class, molecular races like little lines which no longer respond to the great molar oppositions. It is certainly no longer a matter of a synthesis of the two, of a synthesis of 1 and 2, but of a third which always comes from elsewhere and disturbs the binarity of the two, not so much inserting itself in their opposition as in their complementarity. It is not a matter of adding a new segment on to the preceding segments on the line (a third sex, a third class, a third age), but of tracing another line in the middle of the segmentary line, in the middle of the segments, which carries them off according to the variable speeds and slownesses in a movement of flight or of flux. To continue the use of geographical terms: imagine that between *the West and the East* a certain segmentarity is introduced, opposed in a binary machine, arranged in the State apparatuses, overcoded by an abstract machine as the sketch of a World Order. It is then from *North to South* that the destabilization takes place, as Giscard d'Estaing said gloomily, and a stream erodes a path, even if it is a shallow stream, which brings everything into play and diverts the plane of organization. A Corsican here, elsewhere a Palestinian, a plane hijacker, a tribal upsurge, a feminist movement, a Green ecologist, a Russian dissident – there will always be someone to rise up to the south. Imagine the Greeks and the Trojans as two opposed segments, face to face: but look, the Amazons arrive, they begin by overthrowing the Trojans, so that the Greeks cry, 'The Amazons are with us', but they turn against the Greeks, attacking them from behind with the violence of a torrent. This is how Kleist's *Penthesilea* begins. The great ruptures, the great oppositions, are always negotiable; but not the little crack, the imperceptible ruptures which come from the south. We say 'south' without attaching any importance to this. We talk of the south in order to mark a direction which is different from that of the line of segments. But everyone has his south – it doesn't matter where it is – that is, his line of slope or flight. Nations, classes, sexes have their south. Godard: what counts is not merely the two opposed camps on the great line where they confront each other, but also the frontier, through which everything passes and shoots on a broken molecular line of a different orientation. May 1968 was an explosion of such a molecular line, an irruption of the Amazons, a frontier which traced its unexpected line, drawing along the segments like torn-off blocs which have lost their bearings.

We may be criticized for not escaping from dualism, with two kinds of lines, which are cut up, planified, machined, differently. But what defines dualism is not the number of terms, any more than one escapes from dualism by adding other terms (× 2). You only escape dualisms effectively by shifting them like a load, and when you find between the terms, whether they are two or more, a narrow gorge like a border or a frontier which will turn the set into a multiplicity, independently of the number of parts. What we call an assemblage is, precisely, a multiplicity. Now, any assemblage necessarily includes lines of rigid and binary segmentarity, no less than molecular lines, or lines of border, of flight or slope. The devices of power do not seem to us to be exactly constitutive of assemblages, but to form part of them in one dimension on which the whole assemblage can topple over or turn back on itself. But, in fact, in so far as dualisms belong to this dimension, there is another dimension of the assemblage which does not form a dualism with this latter. There is no dualism between abstract overcoding machines and abstract machines of mutation: the latter find themselves segmentarized, organized, overcoded by the others, at the same time as they undermine them; both work within each other at the heart of the assemblage. In the same way there is no dualism between the two planes of transcendent organization and immanent consistence: indeed it is from the forms and subjects of the first plane that the second constantly tears the particles between which there are no longer relationships of speed and slowness, and it is also on the plane of immanence that the other arises, working in it to block movements, fix affects, organize forms and subjects. The speed indicators presuppose forms that they dissolve, no less than the organizations presuppose the material in fusion which they put in order. We do not therefore speak of a dualism between two kinds of 'things', but of a multiplicity of dimensions, of lines and directions in the heart of an assemblage. To the question 'How can desire desire its own repression, how can it desire its slavery?' we reply that the powers which crush desire, or which subjugate it, themselves already form part of assemblages of desire: it is sufficient for desire to follow this particular line, for it to find itself caught, like a boat, under this particular wind. There is no desire *for* revolution, as there is no desire *for* power, desire *to* oppress or *to* be oppressed; but revolution, oppression, power, etc., are the actual component lines of a given assemblage. It is not that these lines are pre-existent; they are traced out, they are formed, immanent to each other, mixed up in each other, at the same time as the assemblage of desire is formed, with its machines tangled up and its planes intersecting. We don't know in advance which one will function as line of gradient, or in what form it will be barred. This is true of a musical assemblage, for example: with its codes and territorialities, its constraints and its apparatuses of power, its dichotomized measures, its melodic and harmonic forms which are developed, its transcendent plane of organization, but also with its transformers of speed between sound molecules, its 'non-pulsed time', its proliferations and dissolutions, its child-becomings, woman-becomings, animal-becomings, its immanent plane of consistence. The long-term role of the power of the church, in musical assemblages, and what the musicians succeed in making pass into this, or into the middle. This is true of all assemblages. What must be compared in each case are the movements of deterritorialization and the processes of reterritorialization which appear in an assemblage. But what do they mean, these words which Félix invents to make them into variable coefficients? We could go back to the commonplaces of the evolution of humanity: man, *deterritorialized animal*. When they say to us that the hominoid removed its front paws from the earth and that the hand is at first locomotor, then prehensile, these are the thresholds or the quanta of deterritorialization, but each time with a complementary reterritorialization: the locomotor hand as the deterritorialized paw is reterritorialized on the branches which it uses to pass from tree to tree; the prehensile hand as deterritorialized locomotion is reterritorialized on the torn-off, borrowed elements called tools that it will brandish or propel. But the 'stick' tool is itself a deterritorialized branch; and the great inventions of man imply a passage to the steppe as deterritorialized forest; at the same time man is reterritorialized on the steppe. The breast is said to be a mammary gland deterritorialized by vertical stature; and the mouth a deterritorialized animal mouth, by the turning-up of the mucous membranes to the exterior: but a correlative reterritorialization is carried out of the lips on to the breast and conversely, so that the bodies and the environments are traversed by very different speeds of deterritorialization, by differential speeds, whose complementarities form continuums of intensity, but also give rise to processes of reterritorialization. At the limit, it is the Earth itself, the deterritorialized ('the desert grows . . .'), and it is the nomad, the man of earth, the man of deterritorialization – although he is also the one who does not move, who remains attached to the environment, desert or steppe.

II

But it is in concrete social fields, at specific moments, that the comparative movements of deterritorialization, the continuums of intensity and the combinations of flux that they form must be studied. We take some examples from around the eleventh century: the movement of flight of monetary masses; the great deterritorialization of peasant masses under the pressure of the latest invasions and the increased demands of the lords; the deterritorialization of the masses of the nobility, which takes forms as varied as the Crusades, settlement in towns, the new types of exploitation of the earth (renting or wage labour); the new forms of towns, whose installations become less and less territorial; the deterritorialization of the Church, with the dispossession of its lands, its 'peace of God', its organization of Crusades; the deterritorialization of woman with chivalric love and then courtly love. The Crusades (including the Children's Crusade) may appear as a threshold of combination of all these movements. One might say in a certain sense that what is primary in a society are the lines, the movements of flight. For, far from being a flight from the social, far from being utopian or even ideological, these constitute the social field, trace out its gradation and its boundaries, the whole of its becoming. A Marxist can be quickly recognized when he says that a society contradicts itself, is defined by its contradictions, and in particular by its class contradictions. We would rather say that, in a society, everything flees and that a society is defined by its lines of flight which affect masses of all kinds (here again, 'mass' is a molecular notion). A society, but also a collective assemblage, is defined first by its points of deterritorialization, its fluxes of deterritorialization. The great geographical adventures of history are lines of flight, that is, long expeditions on foot, on horseback or by boat: that of the Hebrews in the desert, that of Genseric the Vandal crossing the Mediterranean, that of the nomads across the steppe, the long march of the Chinese – it is always on a line of flight that we create, not, indeed, because we imagine that we are dreaming but, on the contrary, because we trace out the real on it, we compose there a plane of consistence. To flee, but in fleeing to seek a weapon.

This primacy of lines of flight must not be understood chronologically, or in the sense of an eternal generality. It is rather the fact and the right of the untimely: a time which is not pulsed, a hecceity like a wind which blows up, a midnight, a midday. For reterritorializations happen at the same time: monetary ones on new circuits; rural ones on new modes of exploitation; urban ones on new functions, etc. To the extent that an accumulation of all these reterritorializations takes place, a 'class' then emerges which benefits particularly from it, capable of homogenizing it and overcoding all its segments. At the limit it would be necessary to distinguish the movements of masses of all kinds, with their respective coefficients of speed, and the stabilizations of classes, with their segments distributed in the reterritorialization of the whole – the same thing acting as mass and as class, but on two different lines which are entangled, with contours which do not coincide. One is then better able to understand why we sometimes say that there are at least three different lines, sometimes only two, sometimes only one which is very muddled. Sometimes three lines because the line of flight or rupture combines all the movements of deterritorialization, precipitates their quanta, tears from them the accelerated particles which come into contact with one another, carries them on to a plane of consistence or a mutating machine; and then a second, molecular line where the deterritorializations are merely relative, always compensated by re-territorializations which impose on them so many loops, detours, of equilibrium and stabilization; finally the molar line with clearly determined segments, where the reterritorial-izations accumulate to form a plane of organization and pass into an overcoding machine. Three lines, one of which would be like the nomadic line, another migrant and the third sedentary (the migrant is not at all the same as the nomadic).

Or else there would be only two lines, because the molecular line would appear only to be oscillating between the two extremes, sometimes carried along by the combination of fluxes of deterritorialization, sometimes brought back to the accumulation of reterritorializations (the migrant sometimes allies with the nomad, sometimes is a mercenary or the federate of an empire: the Ostrogoths and Visigoths). Or else there is only one line, the primary line of flight, of border or frontier, which is relativized in the second line, which allows itself to be stopped or cut in the third. But even then it may be convenient to present THE line as being born from the explosion of the two others. Nothing is more complicated than the line or the lines – it is that which Melville speaks of, uniting the boats in their organized segmentarity, Captain Ahab in his animal and-molecular-becoming, the white whale in its crazy flight. Let us go back to the regimes of signs about which we spoke earlier: how the line of flight is barred under a despotic regime, affected by a negative sign; how it finds in the Hebrews' regime a positive but relative value, cut up into successive processes . . . These were two cases only, briefly outlined, and there are many others: each time it is the essential element of politics. Politics is active experimentation, since we do not know in advance which way a line is going to turn. Draw the line, says the accountant: but one can in fact draw it *anywhere*.

There are so many dangers: each of the three lines has its dangers. The danger of rigid segmentarity or of the cutting line appears everywhere. For this concerns not merely our relationships with the State but all the devices of power which work upon our bodies, all the binary machines which cut us up, the abstract machines which overcode us: it concerns our way of perceiving, acting, feeling, our regimes of signs. It is true that national States oscillate between two poles: when it is liberal, the State is merely an apparatus which directs the realization of the abstract machine; when it is totalitarian it takes upon itself the abstract machine and tends to become indistinguishable from it. But the segments which run through us and through which we pass are, in any case, marked by a rigidity which reassures us, while turning us into creatures which are the most fearful, but also the most pitiless and bitter. The danger is so pervasive and so obvious that we should rather ask ourselves why we need such segmentarity despite all this. Even if we had the power to blow it up, could we succeed in doing so without destroying ourselves, since it is so much a part of the conditions of life, including our organism and our very reason? The prudence with which we must manipulate that line, the precautions we must take to soften it, to suspend it, to divert it, to undermine it, testify to a long labour which is not merely aimed against the State and the powers that be, but directly at ourselves.

All the more so, since the second line has its own dangers. It is certainly not sufficient to attain or to trace out a molecular line, to be carried along a supple line. Here again, everything is involved, our perception, our actions and passions, our regimes of signs. But not only may we discover on a supple line the same dangers as on the rigid one, merely miniaturized, scattered or rather molecularized: little Oedipal communities have replaced the family Oedipus, mobile relationships of force have taken over from the devices of power, cracks have replaced the segregations. There is worse to come: it is the supple lines themselves which produce or encounter their own dangers, a threshold crossed too quickly, an intensity become dangerous because it could not be tolerated. You have not taken enough precautions. This is the 'black hole' phenomenon: a supple line rushes into a black hole from which it will not be able to extricate itself. Guattari discusses micro-fascisms which exist in a social field without necessarily being centralized in a particular apparatus of the State. We have left behind the shores of rigid segmentarity, but we have entered a regime which is no less organized where each embeds himself in his own black hole and becomes dangerous in that hole, with a self-assurance about his own case, his role and his mission, which is even more disturbing than the certainties of the first line: the Stalins of little groups, local law-givers, micro-fascisms of gangs . . . Some have said that we see the schizop'hrenic as the true revolutionary. We believe, rather, that schizophrenia is the descent of a molecular process into a black hole. Marginals have always inspired fear in us, and a slight horror. They are not clandestine enough.

(NOTE: In any case, they scare me. There is a molecular speech of madness, or of the drug addict or the delinquent *in vivo* which is no more valid that the great discourses of a psychiatrist *in vitro*. There is as much self-assurance on the former's part as certainty on the latter's part. It is not the marginals who create the lines; they install themselves on these lines and make them their property, and this is fine when they have that strange modesty of men of the line, the prudence of the experimenter, but it is a disaster when they slip into a black hole from which they no longer utter anything but the micro-fascist speech of their dependency and their giddiness: 'We are the avant-garde', 'We are the marginals.' *G.D.*)

It even happens that the two lines are mutually sustaining and that the organization of a more and more rigid segmentarity on the level of great molar wholes enters on to the same circuit as the management of the little fears and of the black holes into which everyone plunges in the molecular network. Paul Virilio depicts the world State as it is sketched out today: a State of absolute peace still more terrifying than that of total war, having realized its full identity with the abstract machine, and in which the equilibrium of spheres of influence and of great segments intercommunicates with a 'secret capillarity' – where the luminous and clearly dissected city now shelters only nocturnal troglodytes, each embedded in his own black hole, a 'social swamp' which exactly completes the 'obvious and super-organized society'.[6]

And it would be wrong to think that it is sufficient, in the end, to take the line of flight or rupture. First, one must trace it out, know where and how to trace it out. And then it has its own danger, which is perhaps the worst of all. It is not just that lines of flight, the most steeply sloping, risk being barred, segmentarized, drawn into black holes. They have yet another special risk: that of turning into lines of abolition, of destruction, of others and of oneself. A passion for abolition. Just like music – why does it give us the urge to die? Marie's death-cry, stretched out lengthways, floating along the surface of the water, and Lulu's death-cry, vertical and celestial. How is it that all the examples of lines of flight that we have given, even from writers we like, turn out so badly? Lines of flight turn out badly not because they are imaginary, but precisely because they are real and in their reality. They turn out badly not just because they are short-circuited by the two other lines, but on their own account, as a result of a danger which they conceal. Kleist and his suicide pact, Hölderlin and his madness, Fitzgerald and his destruction, Virginia Woolf and her disappearance. One can imagine some of these deaths being peaceful and even happy, the hecceity of a death which is no longer that of a person, but the extraction of a pure event – at its own time, on its own plane. But, indeed, can the plane of immanence, the plane of consistence, only bring us a death which is relatively dignified and without bitterness? It was not made for that. Even if all creation comes to an end in its abolition, which was fashioning it from the start, even if all music is the pursuit of silence, they cannot be judged according to their end or their supposed aim, for they exceed them in all dimensions. When they end up with death, this is a function of a danger which is proper to them, and not of their destination. This is our main point: why on lines of flight, *qua* real, does the 'metaphor' of war recur so frequently, even at the most personal, the most individual level? Hölderlin and the battlefield, Hyperion. Kleist: everywhere in his work is the idea of a war-machine against the apparatuses of the State, but in his own life also is the idea of a war to be waged, which must lead him to suicide. Fitzgerald: 'I had the feeling of standing in the dusk on an abandoned shooting field.' *Criticism and the clinic*: life and work are the same thing, when they have adapted the line of flight which makes them the components of the same war-machine. In these conditions life has for a long time ceased to be personal and the work has ceased to be literary or textual.

War is certainly not a metaphor. Like Félix, we assume that the war-machine has a nature and origin quite different from that of the apparatus of the State. The war-machine would have its origin among the nomadic shepherds, against the imperial sedentary peoples; it implies an arithmetical organization in an open space in which men and animals are distributed, as opposed to the geometrical organization of the State which divides out a closed space (even when the war-machine is related to a geometry, it is a quite different geometry, a sort of Archimedean geometry, a geometry of 'problems', and not of 'theorems' like Euclid's). Conversely, State power does not rest on a war-machine, but on the exercise of binary machines which run through us and the abstract machine which overcodes us: a whole 'police'. The war-machine, on the other hand, is run through with woman-becomings, animal-becomings, the becomings-imperceptible of the warriror (cf. the secret as the invention of the war-machine, as opposed to the 'publicity' of the despot or the man of the State). Dumézil has often emphasized this eccentric position of the warrior in relation to the State. Luc de Heusch shows how the war-machine comes from outside, hurling itself on to an already-developed State which did not include it.[7] In one of his last texts Pierre Clastres explains how the function of war in primitive groups was precisely that of warding off the formation of a State apparatus.[8] One might say that the State apparatus and the war-machine do not belong to the same lines, are not constructed on the same lines: while the State apparatus belongs to the lines of rigid segmentarity, and even conditions them in so far as it realizes their overcoding, the war-machine follows lines of flight and of the steepest gradient, coming from the heart of the steppe or the desert and sinking into the Empire. Genghis Khan and the emperor of China. Military organization is an organization of flight – even the one which Moses gave to his people – not merely because it consists in fleeing something, or even in putting the enemy to flight, but because it traces, wherever it passes, a line of flight or deterritorialization which is at one with its own politics and its own strategy. Under these conditions, one of the most formidable problems which States will have will be that of integrating the war-machine into the form of an institutionalized army, to make it one with their general police (Tamburlaine is perhaps the most striking example of such a conversion). The army is never anything but a compromise. The war-machine may become mercenary or allow itself to be appropriated by the State to the very extent that it conquers it. But there will always be a tension between the State apparatus with its requirement for self-preservation and the war-machine in its undertaking to destroy the State, to destroy the subjects of the State and even to destroy itself or to dissolve itself along the line of flight. If there is no history from the viewpoint of nomads, although everything passes through them, to the point that they are like the *noumena* or the unknowable of history, it is because they cannot be separated from this task of abolition which makes the nomadic empires vanish as if of their own accord, at the same time as the war-machine is either destroyed or passes into the service of the State. In short, each time it is traced by a war-machine, the line of flight is converted into a line of abolition, of destruction of others and of itself. And that is the special danger of this type of line, which mingles with, but is not identical to, the previous dangers. To the extent that each time a line of flight turns into a line of death, we do not invoke an internal impulse of the 'death instinct' type, we invoke another assemblage of desire which brings into play a machine which is objectively or extrinsically definable. It is therefore not metaphorically that each time someone destroys others and destroys himself he has invented on his line of flight his own war-machine:

strindberg's conjugal war-machine, Fitzgerald's alcoholic war-machine . . . All Kleist's work rests on the following observation: there is no longer a war-machine on a grand scale like that of the Amazons, the war-machine is no longer anything more than a dream which itself vanishes and gives way to national armies (*the Prince . of Homburg*); how can one reinvent a new type of war machine (*Michael Kohlhaas*), how can one trace out the line of flight in spite of knowing that it leads us to abolition (suicide pact)? To wage one's own war? How otherwise is one to outmanoeuvre this final trap?

The differences do not pass between the individual and the collective, for we see no duality between these two types of problem: there is no subject of enunciation, but every proper name is collective, every assemblage is already collective. Neither do the differences pass between the natural and the artificial since they both belong to the machine and interchange there. Nor between the spontaneous and the organized, since the only question is one of modes of organization. Nor between the segmentary and the centralized, since centralization is itself an organization which rests on a form of rigid segmentarity. The effective differences pass between the lines, even though they are all immanent to one another, all entangled in one another. This is why the question of schizoanalysis or pragmatics, micro-politics itself, never consists in interpreting, but merely in asking what are your lines, individual or group, and what are the dangers on each.

(1) What are your rigid segments, your binary and overcoding machines? For even these are not given to you ready-made, we are not simply divided up by binary machines of class, sex or age: there are others which we constantly shift, invent without realizing it. And what are the dangers if we blow up these segments too quickly? Wouldn't this kill the organism itself, the organism which possesses its own binary machines, even in its nerves and its brain?

(2) What are your supple lines, what are your fluxes and thresholds? Which is your set of relative deterritorializations

and correlative reterritorializations? And the distribution of black holes: which are the black holes of each one of us, where a beast lurks or a micro-fascism thrives?

(3) What are your lines of flight, where the fluxes are combined, where the thresholds reach a point of adjacence and rupture? Are they still tolerable, or are they already caught up in a machine of destruction and self-destruction which would reconstitute a molar fascism? It may happen that an assemblage of desire and of enunciation is reduced to its most rigid lines, its devices of power. There are assemblages which have only these sorts of lines. But other dangers stalk each of them, more supple and viscous dangers, of which each of us alone is judge, as long as there is still time. The question 'How is it that desire can desire its own repression?' does not give rise to real theoretical difficulty, but to many practical difficulties each time. There is desire as soon as there is a machine or 'body without organs'. But there are bodies without organs like hardened empty envelopes, because their organic components have been blown up too quickly and too violently, an 'overdose'. There are bodies without organs which are cancerous and fascist, in black holes or machines of abolition. How can desire outmanoeuvre all that by managing its plane of immanence and of consistence which each time runs up against these dangers?

There is no general prescription. We have done with all globalizing concepts. Even concepts are heccities, events. What is interesting about concepts like desire, or machine, or assemblage is that they only have value in their variables, and in the maximum of variables which they allow. We are not for concepts as big as hollow teeth, THE law, THE master, THE rebel. We are not here to keep the tally of the dead and the victims of history, the martyrdom of the Gulags, and to draw the conclusion that 'The revolution is impossible, but we thinkers must think the impossible since the impossible only exists through our thought!' It seems to us that there would never have been the tiniest Gulag if the victims had kept up the same discourse as those who weep over them today. The victims would have had to think and live in a quite different way to give substance to those who weep in their name, and who think in their name, and who give lessons in their name. It was their life-force which impelled them, not their bitterness; their sobriety, not their ambition; their anorexia, not their huge appetites, as Zola would have said. We have set out to write a book of life, not of accounts, or of the tribunal even of the people or of pure thought. The question of a revolution has never been utopian spontaneity versus State organization. When we challenge the model of the State apparatus or of the party organization which is modelled on the conquest of that apparatus, we do not, however, fall into the grotesque alternatives: either that of appealing to a state of nature, to a spontaneous dynamic, or that of becoming the self-styled lucid thinker of an impossible revolution, whose very impossibility is such a source of pleasure. The question has always been organizational, not at all ideological: is an organization possible which is not modelled on the apparatus of the State, even to prefigure the State to come? Perhaps a war-machine with its lines of flight? In order to oppose the war-machine to the State apparatus in every assemblage – even a musical or literary one – it would be necessary to evaluate the degree of proximity to this or that pole. But how would a war-machine, in any domain whatever, become modern, and how would it ward off its own fascist dangers, when confronted by the totalitarian dangers of the State, its own dangers of destruction in comparison with the conservation of the State? In a certain way it is very simple, this happens on its own and every day. The mistake would be to say: there is a globalizing State, the master of its plans and extending its traps; and then, a force of resistance which will adopt the form of the State even if it entails betraying us, or else which will fall into local spontaneous or partial struggles, even if it entails being suffocated and beaten every time. The most centralized State is not at all the master of its plans, it is also an experimenter, it performs injections, it is unable to look into the future: the economists of the State declare themselves incapable of predicting the increase in a monetary mass. American politics is forced to proceed by empirical injections, not at all by apodictic programmes. What a sad and sham game is played by those who speak of a supremely cunning Master, in order to present the image of themselves as rigorous, incorruptible and 'pessimist' thinkers. It is along the different lines of complex assemblages that the powers that be carry out their experiments, but along them also arise experimenters of another kind, thwarting predictions, tracing out active lines of flight, looking for the combination of these lines, increasing their speed or slowing it down, creating the plane of consistence fragment by fragment, with a war-machine which would weigh the dangers that it encountered at each step.

What characterizes our situation is both beyond and on this side of the State. *Beyond* national States, the development of a world market, the power of multinational companies, the outline of a 'planetary' organization, the extension of capitalism to the whole social body, clearly forms a great abstract machine which overcodes the monetary, industrial and technological fluxes. At the same time the means of exploitation, control and surveillance become more and more subtle and diffuse, in a certain sense molecular (the workers of the rich countries necessarily take part in the plundering of the Third World, men take part in the over-exploitation of women, etc.). But the abstract machine, with its dysfunctions, is no more infallible than the national States which are not able to regulate them on their own territory and from one territory to another. The State no longer has at its disposal the political, institutional or even financial means which would enable it to fend off the social repercussions of the machine; it is doubtful whether it can eternally rely on the old forms like the police, armies, bureaucracies, even trade union bureaucracies, collective installations, schools, families.

Enormous land slides are happening *on this side of* the state, following lines of gradient or of flight, affecting principally:

(1) the marking out of territories; (2) the mechanisms of economic subjugation (new characteristics of unemployment, of inflation); (3) the basic regulatory frameworks (crisis of the school, of trade unions, of the army, of women . . .); (4) the nature of the demands which become qualitative as much as quantitative ('quality of life' rather than the 'standard of living').

All this constitutes what can be called a *right to desire*. It is not surprising that all kinds of minority questions – linguistic, ethnic, regional, about sex, or youth – resurge not only as archaisms, but in up-to-date revolutionary forms which call once more into question in an entirely immanent manner both the global economy of the machine and the assemblages of national States. Instead of gambling on the eternal impossibility of the revolution and on the fascist return of a warmachine in general, why not think that *a new type of revolution is in the course of becoming possible*, and that all kinds of mutating, living machines conduct wars, are combined and trace out a plane of consistence which undermines the plane of organization of the World and the States?[9] For, once again, the world and its States are no more masters of their plane than revolutionaries are condemned to the deformation of theirs. Everything is played in uncertain games, 'front to front, back to back, back to front . . .'. The question of the future of the revolution is a bad question because, in so far as it is asked, there are so many people who do not *become* revolutionaries, and this is exactly why it is done, to impede the question of the revolutionary-becoming of people, at every level, in every place.

5

The Actual and the Virtual[1]

Translated by Eliot Ross Albert[2]

I

Philosophy is the theory of multiplicities, each of which is composed of actual and virtual elements. Purely actual objects do not exist. Every actual surrounds itself with a cloud of virtual images. This cloud is composed of a series of more or less extensive coexisting circuits, along which the virtual images are distributed, and around which they run.[3] These virtuals vary in kind as well as in their degree of proximity from the actual particles by which they are both emitted and absorbed. They are called virtual in so far as their emission and absorption, creation and destruction, occur in a period of time shorter than the shortest continuous period imaginable; it is this very brevity that keeps them subject to a principle of uncertainty or indetermination. The virtuals, encircling the actual, perpetually renew themselves by emitting yet others, with which they are in turn surrounded and which go on in turn to react upon the actual: 'in the heart of the cloud of the virtual there is a virtual of a yet higher order ... every virtual particle surrounds itself with a virtual cosmos and each in its turn does likewise indefinitely.'[4] It is the dramatic identity of their dynamics that makes a perception resemble a particle: an actual perception surrounds itself with a cloud of virtual images, distributed on increasingly remote, increasingly large, moving circuits, which both make and unmake each other. These are memories of different sorts, but they are still called virtual images in that their speed or brevity subjects them too to a principle of the unconsciousness. It is by virtue of their mutual inextricability that virtual images are able to react upon actual objects. From this perspective, the virtual images delimit a continuum, whether one takes all of the circles together or each individually, a spatium determined in each case by the maximum of time imaginable. The varyingly dense layers of the actual object correspond to these, more or less extensive, circles of virtual images. These layers, whilst themselves virtual, and upon which the actual object becomes itself virtual, constitute the total impetus of the object.[5] The plane of immanence, upon which the dissolution of the actual object occurs, is itself constituted when both object and image are virtual. But the process of actualization undergone by the actual is one which has as great an effect on the image as it does on the object. The continuum of virtual images is fragmented and the spatium cut up according to whether the temporal decompositions are regular or irregular. The total impetus of the virtual object splits into forces corresponding to the partial continuum, and the speeds traversing the cut-up spatium.[6] The virtual is never independent of the singularities which cut it up and divide it out on the plane of immanence. As Leibniz has shown, force is as much a virtual in the process of being actualized as the space through which it travels. The plane is therefore divided into a multiplicity of planes according to the cuts in the continuum, and to the divisions of force which mark the actualization of the virtual. But all the planes merge into one following the path which leads to the actual. The plane of immanence includes both the virtual and its actualization simultaneously, without there being any assignable limit between the two. The actual is the complement or the product, the object of actualization, which has nothing but the virtual as its subject. Actualization belongs to the virtual. The actualization of the virtual is singularity whereas the actual itself is individuality constituted. The actual falls from the plane like a fruit, whilst the actualization relates it back to the plane as if to that which turns the object back into a subject.

II

Thus far we have considered those cases in which the actual is surrounded by increasingly extensive, remote and diverse virtualities: a particle creates ephemera, a perception evokes memories. But the inverse movement also occurs: in which, as the circles contract, the virtual draws closer to the actual, both become less and less distinct. You get to an inner circuit which links only the actual object and its virtual image: an actual particle has its virtual double, which barely diverges from it at all; an actual perception has its own memory as a sort of immediate, consecutive or even simultaneous double.[7] For, as Bergson shows, memory is not an actual image which forms after the object has been perceived, but a virtual image coexisting with the actual perception of the object. Memory is a virtual image contemporary with the actual object, its double, its 'mirror image',[8] as in *The Lady from Shanghai*, in which the mirror takes control of a character, engulfs him and leaves him as just a virtuality; hence, there is coalescence and division, or rather oscillation, a perpetual exchange between the actual object and its virtual image: the virtual image never stops becoming actual. The virtual image absorbs all of a character's actuality, at the same time as the actual character is no more than a virtuality. This perpetual exchange between the virtual and the actual is what defines a crystal; and it is on the plane of immanence that crystals appear. The actual and the virtual coexist, and enter into a tight circuit which we are continually retracing from one to the other. This is no longer a singularization, but an individuation as process, the actual and its virtual: no longer an actualization but a crystallization. Pure virtuality no longer has to actualize itself, since it is a strict correlative of the actual with which it forms the tightest circuit. It is not so much that one cannot assign the terms 'actual' and 'virtual' to distinct objects, but rather that the two are indistinguishable. The actual object and the virtual image, the object become virtual, the image actual, are all figures dealt with in elementary optics.[9] This distinction between the virtual and the actual corresponds to the most fundamental split in time, that is to say, the differentiation of its passage into two great jets: the passing of the present, and the preservation of the past. The present is a variable given measured in continuous time, a supposedly mono-directional movement, in which the present passes up until the exhaustion of that time.[10] The actual is defined by this passing of the present. But the virtual's ephemerality appears in a smaller space of time than that which marks the minimum movement in a single direction. This is why the virtual is 'ephemeral', but the virtual also preserves the past, since that ephemerality is continually making minute adjustments in response to changes of direction. The period of time which is smaller than the smallest period of continuous time imaginable in one direction is also the longest time, longer than the longest unit of continuous time imaginable in all directions. The passing of the present, the preservation and self-preservation of the ephemeral each occur according to their own scale of measurement. Virtuals communicate directly over the top of the actuals which separate them. The two aspects of time, the actual image of the present which passes and the virtual image of the past which is preserved, are distinguishable during actualization although they have unassignable limits, but exchange during crystallization to the extent that they become indiscernible, each relating to the role of the other.

The relationship between the actual and the virtual takes the form of a circuit, but it does so in two ways: sometimes the actual refers to the virtuals as to other things in the vast circuits where the virtual is actualized; sometimes the actual refers to the virtual as its own virtual, in the smallest circuits where the virtual crystallizes with the actual. The plane of immanence contains both actualization as the relationship of the virtual with other terms, and even the actual as a term with which the virtual is exchanged. In any case, the relationship between the actual and the virtual is not the same as that established between two actuals. Actuals imply already constituted individuals, and are ordinarily determined, whereas the relationship of the actual and the virtual forms an acting individuation or a highly specific and remarkable singularization which needs to be determined case by case.

6

Pericles and Verdi:
The Philosophy of François Châtelet
Translated by Joseph Hughes

François Châtelet has always defined himself as a rationalist, but there are many kinds of rationalism. He frequently alludes to Plato, to Hegel, and to Marx. However, above all he is an Aristotelian. What distinguishes him from a Thomist? Without a doubt it is the manner in which he rejects God and all transcendence. All transcendence, all beliefs in another world, he calls presumptions (*outre-cuidances*). Never before has there been a philosophy more tranquilly atheist (with the exception of Nietzsche's, of course). A tranquil atheism is a philosophy for which God is not a problem. The non-existence or even the death of God are not problems but rather the conditions one must have already acquired in order to make the true problems surge forth: there is no other modesty. Never before has philosophy established itself so firmly in a pure field of immanence.

In our philosophical jargon, we call transcendence a principle posed both as a source of all explanation and as a superior reality. The word has a nice ring to it and I find it fitting. The presumptuous, small or large, from the leader of a small group to that of the president of the United States, from a psychiatrist to a CEO can only function by recourse (*coups*) to transcendence – just as a drunk might get by through sips (*coups*) of red wine. The medieval God has spread himself thin, without losing his strength or his profound formal unity. Science, the Working Class, the Motherland, Progress, Health, Defense, Democracy, Socialism – the list would be too long – are all among his avatars. These transcendences, which exercise with a heightened ferocity their labors of organization and extermination, have taken his place (to such a degree that we can say he is still there, omnipresent).

(*Les années de démolition*, p. 263)

Immanence, the field of immanence, consists of a Potential-Act relation.[1] The two notions are inseparable and exist only in correlation. It is in this that Châtelet is Aristotelian. First of all, he experiences a sort of fascination with potential: man is potential, man is matter *(matière)*:

I'm not interested in political power *(pouvoir)*. For me, the contra-power, the anti-power are traps. What interests me is potential, that which makes power power. Now, strictly speaking, potential lies in the ordinary person. I take pleasure in exercising my potential – in doing what I can *(pouvoir)* – to understand and unveil the mechanisms of the capitation of potential wherever I have 'information' – perhaps only to maintain my taste for potential, to keep it alive in me, and to awaken, reawaken, this potential around me. Potential has also been called freedom.

(*Chronique des idées perdues*, p. 218)

But how do we proceed to the act? What is the act of this potential? The act is reason, but we must understand that reason is a process, not a faculty, and that it consists precisely in actualizing a potential or in forming a matter *(matière)*. Because we have no motive to think of either the act or the matter as unique, there is a pluralism of reason. A process of rationalization is thus defined, or invented, each time human relations are established in any matter whatever, in any collection *(ensemble)* whatever, in any multiplicity whatever. The act itself, being a relation, is always political. Reason as a process is political. This can be in the city, but in other groups as well, in small groups, or in me, in nothing other than myself. Psychology, or rather the only supportable psychology, is a politics because I always have to create human relations with myself. There is not a psychology, but a politics of the self (*moi*). There is no metaphysics, but a politics of being. No science, but a politics of matter since man is burdened by matter itself. Even illness: one must 'manage' it when it cannot be overcome and impose upon it human relations. Take, for example, a sonorous matter: the scale or rather a scale is a process of rationalization which consists in establishing human relations in this matter in such a way that it actualizes its potential and becomes human. Marx analyzed the sense organs from this point of view in order to show through them a man-Nature immanence: the ear becomes the human ear when the sonorous object becomes musical. It is the extremely diverse set of processes of rationalization which constitutes the becoming or the activity of man, the Praxis or praxes. We cannot tell whether a human unity exists, in this respect, from either the historical point of view or the general point of view.

Is there a properly human matter, a pure potential which is distinct from the act and capable of fascinating us? It would not be our freedom if it did not at the same time appear as its opposite, 'capitation', as Châtelet said above. This would be an obtuse act of potential as opposed to an act capable of realization, an inverse of reason, or even more than an opposite – a privation or an alienation. It is as if there were a non-human relation interior or immanent to the human relation itself, an inhumanity proper to man. Freedom becomes man's capacity to defeat man, but also to be defeated. Potential is pathos, that is, passivity, receptivity. But receptivity is first of all the potential to give and receive blows – a strange endurance. One can always write the history of systems of domination and the activities of masters, but these would be nothing without the desire of those who in the name of the blows which they receive aspire to give them back. They fight for their servitude as if it were their freedom, said Spinoza. So much so that whether it is exercised or suffered, power (*pouvoir*) is not only the activity of man's social existence but also the passivity of his natural existence. A unity of war and earth, such as Châtelet found traces of in Claude Simon. Or even in Marxism, which has never separated the active existence of historical man from the passive existence of a natural being which is its double:

> Reason and its irrationality was Marx's theme, and it is ours. . . . It wants to be a critical science of effective passivity, the land-tax of humanity. Man does not die because he is mortal (no more than he lies because he is 'dishonest' or loves because he is 'amorous'). He dies because he doesn't eat enough, because he is reduced to the state of a beast, because he is killed. Historical materialism reminds us of these facts, and in *Capital*, Marx lays the foundations of a method which could allow the analysis of the mechanisms that govern, during a given epoch (a particularly revelatory epoch for that matter), the fact of passivity.
>
> (*Questions, Objections*, p. 115)

Are there not values proper to pathos, even if only that despair of the world which is so present in Châtelet beneath an extreme politeness? Men are continually destroying (*démolir*) one another to such an extent that it might seem better to destroy oneself in agreeable or even fictional circumstances. 'Of course all life is a process of breaking down (*un processus de démolition*)', Fitzgerald said, and this 'of course' resounds as a guarantee of immanence: this non-human relation in the relation with oneself.[2] Châtelet's sole novel, *Les années de démolition*, exhibits a profoundly Fitzgeraldian inspiration, an

elegance in disaster. It is not a question of dying, or of a desire to die, but of investing the temptation to die in a sublime
element like music. And again, this is not a psychoanalytic
affair, but a political one. One must take into account this
vector of destruction which is able to traverse a collectivity
or a man, Athens or Pericles. *Périclès*: this was Châtelet's first
book. For Châtelet, Pericles will always be the image of the
great man or hero, even in his 'passivity', even in his failure
which will become the failure of democracy, even in following the disquieting vector.

Pathos has a second value: politeness – in truth a Greek
politeness which would already be the sketch or outline of
human relations and the beginnings of an act of reason.
Human relations begin with a metric or an organization of
space which holds the city together. It is an art of establishing the right distances between men, not hierarchical but
geometrical, so that they are neither too close nor too far
and are unable to exchange blows. It makes the encounter
between men a rite, a sort of ritual of immanence, even if
a little schizophrenia is necessary. The Greeks have taught
us, as Gernet and Vernant have shown, to not nail ourselves
down to an established center, but to acquire the capacity to
carry the center with ourselves in order to organize groups
(*ensembles*) of symmetrical and reversible relations effectu-
ated by free men. Perhaps this is not enough to overcome
the despair of the world: there are less and less polite men,
and it takes at least two to be polite. The extreme politeness
of François Châtelet, however, is itself nothing more than a
mask for a third value of pathos which we could call kindness
or affectionate benevolence. Perhaps this is not the most suitable name, but this quality, this value, belonged profoundly
to Châtelet. More than a value or a quality, however, it is a
disposition of thought, an act of thought.

It consists in this: to not know in advance how someone will
eventually find himself capable of establishing in and outside

of himself a process of rationalization. There are of course all of the lost cases (despair), and perhaps we are all born on a ground of demolition. But we never pass up a chance to get out. When an opportunity presents itself, what would we have to do in order to escape our demolitions? There is no pure Reason or rationality par excellence. There are only heterogeneous processes of rationalization which are very different depending on the different domains, epochs, groups, and people. They never stop aborting, sliding, getting into impasses, but also pulling themselves together elsewhere, with new measures, new rhythms, new attitudes. The plurality of processes of rationalization have already been the object of basic epistemological analyses (Koyré, Bachelard, Canguilhem) and sociopolitical analyses (Max Weber). And in his last books Foucault oriented this pluralism towards an analysis of human relations which would have constituted the project of a new ethics from the point of view of what he called 'processes of subjectification.' He showed the bifurcations, the derivations, the shattered history of a reason which was always in a state of liberation or alienation in the relations of man with himself. And it was necessary for Foucault to go all the way back to the Greeks not in order to find once and for all the miracle, the miserable miracle, of reason par excellence, but only in order to diagnose there perhaps the first rough sketch of a process of rationalization from which many others followed under different conditions and different attitudes. Foucault no longer defined the Greek city according to the organization of a new space, but by a human relation determinable as a rivalry between free men or citizens (in politics, but also in love, gymnastics, justice . . .): in the prolongation of a rationalization and a subjectification a free man could only govern other free men, in principle, if he was able to govern himself. Such is the properly Greek act or process which is not a founding act but a singular event in a shattered chain. It is without a doubt here that Châtelet, who for his part had taken the Greek city as his point of departure, encounters Foucault. It is the idea of magistracy which allows Châtelet to define the Greek city not only in its difference from other notions (the priest, the imperial functionary . . .) but also in its correlates which enter into corresponding processes of rationalization (the lottery for example). Nobody has demonstrated as well as Châtelet how the lottery is caught up in a movement of reason. For Châtelet rationalization is a historical and political process which experienced, through Athens, its first event, but also, in Pericles, its defeat and effacement from which further events caught in other processes would break away. Athens was not the advent of an eternal reason, but the singular event of a provisional rationalization, all the more dazzling.

Whenever we affirm one unique reason, universal by right, we fall precisely into what Châtelet calls 'presumption' – a sort of metaphysical impoliteness. He discovered this first in Plato, but even when we recognize in reason a human and only human faculty, a faculty of the ends of man, we uphold in it a transcendence which is still theological. Instead of a pluralism of processes, we erect a dualism which opposes discourse to violence, as though violence did not continue to build a home in discourse itself and furnish it with so many meanderings and motivations. Châtelet had long believed, under the profound influence of Eric Weil, in the opposition of violence and discourse following a Platonic and Hegelian model. But he discovered, to the contrary, the aptitude of discourse to make the inhumanity proper to man speak: it is up to discourse to engage the process of its own rationalization, but only in a becoming, under the pressure of certain motives, on behalf of certain events. What makes *La naissance de l'histoire* so important is that in it Châtelet creates an image of discourse or logos closer to Thucydides than to Plato or Hegel. And he always rejects the two corollaries of a doctrine of universal reason: the utopian demand to invoke an ideal city or a universal state by right, which always turns back against democratic becomings;

the apocalyptic demand to assign a deviation, a fundamental alienation to reason which would be produced once and for all and would reunite in one blow all violence or the non-human. The same 'presumption' (*outre-cuidance*) confers a transcendence upon reason and its corruption, and, since Plato, doubles the one with the other.

Châtelet develops a rational empiricism, or an empirical and pluralist rationalism. What he calls 'empirical' (*empirie*) depends primarily on two negative principles: the abstract does not explain, but must itself be explained; the universal does not exist, but only the singular, singularity, exists. 'Singularity' is not the individual, it is the case, the event, the potential (*potential*), or rather, the distribution of potentials in a given matter. To draw a political map of an individual, of a group or of a society is essentially the same thing: it is a question of prolonging a singularity all the way to the neighborhood of another so that a 'configuration of events' is produced, that is, the richest or most consistent set (*ensemble*) possible. We could do this as historians: for example, the history of Athens. But we are only historians if we know how to recapture the operation that Pericles himself made, that connection, that conjunction of singularities which would remain latent and isolated without a politics to which we rightly give the name Pericles. An individual, even insignificant, is himself one such field of singularities who receives his proper name only from the operations that he undertakes upon himself and in a neighborhood in order to draw from them a prolongable configuration. Châtelet said of himself: I have a petit bourgeois education, I was influenced by Hegel, I lived in one of those historical periods which sickens any somewhat sensitive soul. Here are three facts, 'without relation it seems. In short they form a plural ensemble, the display of something from which it is impossible to tell whether it could be somebody.' What we will call empirical (*empirie*), or *history in the present*, is independent of the importance of the considered matter. It is neither the 'lived', which takes pleasure in singularities for themselves and leaves them stranded, nor the 'concept', which drowns them in the universal and turns them into simple moments. It is the operation that emits a veritable throw of the dice in order to produce the most consistent configuration, the curve that determines the most singularities in a potential (*potential*). It is an act of 'deployment' that weaves from one point to another just as many human relations. It is an actualization of potential (*puissance*) or a *becoming active*, a matter of life and its continuation, of reason and its processes, and a victory over death, since there is no other immortality than this history in the present, no other life than that which makes neighborhoods connect and converge. Châtelet will call it 'decision', and his whole philosophy is a philosophy of decision, of the singularity of decision in opposition to the universals of reflection, communication. . . . Whether in my room or in Athens, all action is 'periclean', and 'deep down that which pertains to periclean action is a decision.'

> The weight of the empirical (*empirique*) imposes itself implacably as multiplicity or, more exactly, as a plural ensemble. Empirical (*empirique*). We could just as well say historical, though not in the sense of the work of a historian who as a result of a demand or need for objectivity must keep at a distance and constitute an object he treats as past, but in the sense of a history in the present. Thus, for me, the field in which this discussion situates itself is the empirical *(empirique)*, this being understood as opposing itself at once to the lived — by nature, inessential — and to the conceptual — which belongs to another register.
>
> (*Chronique des idées perdues*, p. 15)

A process of rationalization thus presents itself: it is to actualize a potential, to become active, to produce a human relation, to prolong singularities, to decide. In short, it is to create movement. Are all of these expressions equivalent? In invoking the concrete, philosophers have always claimed to 'create movement' rather than to think it in the abstraction of the universal. The universal has never run nor swam, but has always only run in place or made the movements of swimming on dry sand because it is only occupied with ends. The act of a singular reason is completely different. It leaps into the immanence of life because it gives itself its own motives (*mobiles*). 'If it were possible to construct the image of such a man', the citizen of the universal state, 'it would not be necessary to act politically, and it would suffice, at least imaginarily, to construct his imaginary representation: the problem is not that of ends, but of movement' (*Questions, Objections*, p. 271). Movement is the act itself of potential. To proceed to the act is to make movement, to establish the human relation. To decide is not to want to make the movement, but to make it. It is true that not all movement is a process of rationalization, and, if Châtelet is profoundly Aristotelian, it is because he gives to the distinction between *natural movement* and *forced movement* an exemplary practical and historical range. Forced movement always comes from on high, from a transcendence which gives it an end, from a 'mediation' of abstract thought which appoints its trajectory and which always recomposes it with straight lines even before having undertaken the movement; it does not make claims for a supposedly universal Reason without entering at the same time into a disaster which affects the universe, until we start all over again, just as abstractly, just as fatally. It is the contrary of natural movement, which is only composed of singularities and only accumulates neighborhoods, deploying itself in a space which it creates commensurate to its detours or its inflections, proceeding by connections which are never preestablished, going from the collective to the individual and inversely, from the interior to the exterior and inversely, from the voluntary to the involuntary and inversely. Exploration of neighborhoods, emission of singularities, decision, these are all the act of reason. If reason can be considered a natural faculty, it is precisely as process only insofar as it finds itself in 'movements that are completely singular, produced by entangled trajectories', constructing a 'voluminous space which arises, advances, folds back on itself, spreads itself out, annihilates itself, weakens, explodes' (*Chronique des idées perdus*, p. 237).

> More and more it seems to me that the disasters, the great misfortunes, happen at the moment when forced movements prevail in quantity and in quality over natural movements. A migration of population due to demographic or climatic factors is, in general, less deadly – or less disturbing in any case – than the decided expeditions of the presumptuous like Peter the Hermit, Urban II, or Pizarro. The insurrections engendered by physical and moral misery were the first revolutionary actions of France in 1789. The worker or nationalist interventions of the nineteenth century, the Russian insurrections of 1905, of February and October 1917 were all, in my eyes, examples of natural movement or modes of interior migration in societies which carry individuals on their slopes. The brutes have always introduced their presumptuous force here in order to frustrate or seize these superb and joyous dynamisms, in order to *force* them, in order to transform them into an affair, and if possible an affair of the State. So they recommence the slaughter and recreate institutions, that is, the means of domestication, of imperceptible massacres.
>
> (*Les années de démolition*, p. 255–56)

François Châtelet has always lived in the neighborhood of music. But for Châtelet music was activity itself and not a 'sonorous ground' for the listener. He recognized in music two characteristics: it delivered us neither time nor the eternal, but produced movement; it affirmed neither the lived nor the concept, but constituted the act of sensible Reason. Without a doubt, it is not a question of Wagner, too infatuated with transcendence, too caught up in forced movements, too engaged in the Universal and the universalization of destruction, but of Mozart and of Italian opera, of Verdi. Above all, Châtelet would have loved an opera by Verdi on Pericles. Music seemed to him the most extraordinary decision, always repeated, always to be recaptured. And Châtelet's pages on music are themselves extraordinary because they give us the very tonality of his thought, up until the last moment. Musical art has, as it were, two aspects: the one like a dance of sonorous molecules which reveal the 'materiality of movements ordinarily attributed to the soul', acting upon the whole body that it deploys as its stage, and the other like the creation of human relations in this sonorous matter, which directly produces the affects that are ordinarily explained by psychology. In Verdi a powerful (*puissante*) vocal harmony consists in chords which determine the affect, whereas the melody gains in movements which lead the whole matter: music is a politics. Without soul and without transcendence, material and relational, music is the most reasonable activity of man. Music makes, and makes us make, movement. It maintains our neighborhood and populates it with singularities. It reminds us that reason functions not in order to represent but to actualize potential, in other words, to establish human relations in a (sonorous) matter. This is the very definition of opera. Further, it is through music that one is able to understand, in the end, the meaning of the two words '*historical materialism.*'

> It is as a surface unfolding itself, composed of differences in level and degree that the musical composition is effective. It has no effect of depth, unless in the material sense where it comes about by burrowing into the body and flexing its muscles. It is no more a mastery or a game of time than painting is a technique

of two-dimensional space or sculpture of three-dimensional space. Of course it can produce the impression of the duration which flows, of the event which bursts, or of stagnation. This is only, however, one aspect. The metaphors that I have just used all share a common defect: they situate the musical effect in the domain of representation. But music neither presents nor represents anything, not even apparently. It has this privilege: to render sensible by means of its artifices the impact of sonorous qualities and their combinations on the entire surface of the body including its so-called profound parts . . .

I have often alluded to the project of a physics of quality, of a coordinated and non-systematic ensemble of knowledge aiming to clarify practical relations beyond the ontological distinctions of mind and matter, the anthropological of man and world, the epistemological of idea and thing. Now it seems to me that the work of art, insofar as it sinks its roots into *techne*, that it is a *praxis* – in the Aristotelian sense of the word, that is to say, an imitation-transformation of that on which it works – insofar as it is a work, produces the artificial realities which are the elements of this physics. At the heart of this research, musical art distinguishes itself in that, excluding by nature visual representation and by consequence the specular-speculative trap, it goes very far in this enterprise of the construction of these *automatons* that have the power (*puissance*) of pleasure and strength (*force*) of exploration. . . .

It has this virtue: to act through a subtle matter, to render sensible the materiality of movements that are ordinarily attributed to the soul. It is this that gives reality and strength to the elementary psychology of Giuseppe Verdi's heroes. For the same reason, Mozart's musical phrases impose what the genius of Molière could only suggest: the vehemence of Elvira's desire for Don Giovanni. The fear, the carnal passion, the hate which reflexive or scientific psychology laboriously deduces or induces, music makes exist in their singular situations.

(*Chronique des idées perdues*, p. 237–241)

Notes

Preface

1 Translators' note: in English in the original.

Translators' Introduction

1 Gilles Deleuze and Félix Guattari, *A Thousand Plateaus*, Introduction, The Athlone Press, 1987.
2 English translation, London: The Athlone Press, 1983.
3 English translation, Minneapolis: University of Minnesota Press, 1985.
4 English translation, Introduction to *A Thousand Plateaus*, The Athlone Press, 1987.
5 English translation, The Athlone Press, forthcoming.
6 Vincennes seminar, 7 March 1978.
7 See 'Rhizome', translated by Paul Patton, *I & C*, no. 8, Spring 1981, p. 50.
8 See p. 127, below.

Chapter 1

1 Marcel Proust, *By Way of Sainte-Beuve*, trans. Sylvia Townsend Warner, London: Chatto & Windus, 1958, pp. 194–5.
2 Friedrich W. Nietzsche, 'Schopenhauer Educator', in *Untimely Meditations*, trans. R. J. Hollingdale, Cambridge: Cambridge University Press, 1983, p. 159.
3 Bob Dylan, *Writings and Drawings*, St Albans: Panther, 1974, pp. 168–70.
4* Translators' note: the three phrases in inverted commas are in English in the original.
5* Translators' note: in other words, civil servants.
6* Translators' note: the third essay in his *Untimely Meditations*, op. cit.
7* Translators' note: as described on p. xii, the French *mot d'ordre* is usually translated as 'slogan'. In this context it could be rendered as

'command' or 'command function'. Professor Deleuze wishes to retain the connection with language and expressions such as 'password'.

8* Translators' note: in English in the original.

9* Translators' note: '*Du côté de chez*'. An oblique reference to Proust's *Du Côté de Chez Swann*, usually translated as 'Swann's Way', but literally, 'In the direction of Swann'.

10* Translators' note: Gilles Deleuze, *Différence et Répétition*, Paris: PUF, 1968.

11* Translators' note: Michel Foucault, *L'Ordre du Discours*, Paris: Gallimard, 1971; translated by R. Swyer as 'The Discourse on Language', appendix to *The Archaeology of Knowledge*, New York: Harper & Row, 1972.

12 cf. G. G. Simpson, *L'Evolution et sa signification*, Paris: Payot, 1951.

13 Henry Miller, *Hamlet*, Paris: Correa, p. 49.

Chapter 2

1 cf. The whole analysis of Leslie Fiedler, *The Return of the Vanishing American*, London: Jonathan Cape, 1968.

2 A. Toynbee, *A Study of History*, London: Oxford University Press, 1972, pp. 132 ff.

3 D. H. Lawrence, *Studies in Classic American Literature*, Harmondsworth: Penguin, 1971, pp. 146–7.

4 F. Scott Fitzgerald, *The Crack-Up, with other Pieces and Stories*, Harmondsworth: Penguin, 1965, pp. 52–3.

5 Steven Rose, *The Conscious Brain*, London: Weidenfeld & Nicolson, 1973.

6* Translators' note: for a discussion of the key role of the concept of *délire* in Deleuze's work see Jean-Jacques Lecercle, *Philosophy through the Looking-Glass*, London: Hutchinson, 1985, especially Chapter 5.

7 Lawrence, op. cit., p. 140. And on the double turning-away, cf. Hölderlin's *Remarques sur Oedipe*, with commentaries by Jean Beaufret, Paris: UGE, 1965. And *Jonas*, trans. J. Lindon, Paris: Minuit, 1955.

8 Jacques Besse, *La grande Paque*, Paris: Belfond, 1969.

9* Translators' note: in English in the original.

10 Henry Miller, *Tropic of Cancer*, St Albans: Panther, 1966, pp. 110–11.

11* Translators' note: the phrase *les poètes maudits* literally 'the accursed poets') was coined by Paul Verlaine in 1884 in a brochure about three symbolist poets, Mallarmé, Rimbaud and Tristan Corbière.

12 Lawrence, op. cit.; cf. the whole chapter on Whitman, which opposes sympathy to identification.

13 Henry Miller, *Sexus*, St Albans: Panther, 1970, p. 19.

14* Translators' note: in English in the original.

15 cf. the remarks of François Regnault in the Preface to the translation of *Baladin du monde occidental*, ed. Le Graphe.

16 cf. J.L. Dillard's book on *Black English*, New York: Random House, 1972. And on the problem of languages in South Africa, see Breytenbach, *Feu Froid*, Paris: Bourgois, 1976.

17* Translators' note: in English in the original.

18* Translators' note: *manque-à-être* is a neologism created by Lacan which means, literally, 'lack-to-be'. Lacan himself has suggested 'want to be' as an English rendering: see his *The Four Fundamental Concepts of Psycho-Analysis*, translated by Alan Sheridan, Harmondsworth: Penguin, 1979, p. 281.

19 Joe Bosquet, *Traduit du silence*, Paris: Gallimard, and *Les Capitales*, Paris: Cercle du livre. And Blanchot's wonderful discussions of the event, notably in *L'Espace littéraire*, Paris: Gallimard, 1955.

20 cf. L. White's study of the stirrup and the feudal system, *Technologie médiévale et transformations sociales*, Paris: Mouton.

21 On all these problems, see M. Dobb, *Studies in the Development of Capitalism*, London: Routledge, 1946, chapters 1 and 3.

22* Translators' note: in English in the original.

Chapter 3

1 E. A. Bennett, *Ce que Jung a vraiment dit*, Paris: Gérard, 1973, p. 80.

2* Translators' note: in English in the original.

3* Translators' note: see Chapter 2, note 18.

4 Serge Leclaire, *Démasquer le réel*, Paris: Seuil, 1971, p. 35.

5 cf. the famous case of President Schreber and the verdict which grants him his rights. [Translators' note: the reference is to Freud's essay, 'Psychoanalytic Notes on an Autobiographical Account of a Case of Paranoia (Dementia Paranoides)', in Volume 9 of the Pelican Freud Library, *Case Histories II*, Harmondsworth: Penguin, 1979.]

6 cf. Robert Castel, *Le Psychanalysme*, Paris: François Maspéro, 1973.

7 cf. a curious text of J. A. Miller in *Ornicar*, no. 1.

8 Jacques Donzelot, in *The Policing of Families*, trans. R. Hurley, London: Hutchinson, 1980, shows that psychoanalysis has evolved from the private relationship and that it perhaps entered the 'social' sector very much earlier than has been thought.

9* Translators' note: 'hecceity' is a term from scholastic philosophy which is sometimes rendered as 'thisness'. Professor Deleuze has suggested the following note as explanation of the term: '*Haecceitas* is a term frequently used in the school of Duns Scotus, in order to designate the individuation of beings. Deleuze uses it in a more special sense: in the sense of an individuation which is not that of an object, nor of a person, but rather of an event (wind, river, day or even hour of the day).

Deleuze's thesis is that all individuation is in fact of this type. This is the thesis developed in *Mille Plateaux* with Félix Guattari.'

10 Hecceity – and also longitude, latitude – are excellent medieval concepts, whose analysis was taken as far as possible by certain theologians, philosophers and physicists. We are entirely in their debt in this respect, even if we use these concepts in a different sense.

11 cf. the article of Roland Barthes on Schumann, 'Rasch', in *Language, discours, société*, Seuil, pp. 218 ff.

12* Translators' note: the original is, literally, 'Oh, I could tell you, mummy', a line from a French nursery rhyme.

13 René Nellie, in *L'Erotique des Troubadours*, Tours, 1963, gives a good analysis of this plane of immanence of courtly love, in the way it challenges the interruptions that pleasure would like to introduce into it. In a quite different assemblage, similar utterances and techniques are to be found in Taoism for the construction of a plane of immanence of desire (cf. R. Van Gulik, *Sexual Life in Ancient China*, Leiden: E. J. Brill, 1961, and the commentaries of J.–F. Lyotard, *Economie Libidinale*, Paris: Minuit, 1974).

14 D. H. Lawrence, *Eros et les chiens*, Paris: Bourgois, 1970, p. 290.

15' Malcolm Bradbury, *The Machineries of Joy*, St Albans: Panther, 1977, pp. 38–9.

16 Jean Paris, *L'Espace et le regard*, Paris: Seuil, 1965.

17 cf. the crucial book of W. Labov, *Sociolinguistic Patterns*, Philadelphia: University of Pennsylvania Press, 1972.

18 Pierre Guiraud, *Le Testament de Villon, ou le gai savoir de la basoche*, Paris: Gallimard, 1970.

19 Louis Wolfson, *Le Schizo et les langues*, Paris: Gallimard, 1970. [Translators' note: this book has an introduction by Deleuze. For a discussion of Wolfson see Lecercle, *Philosophy through the Looking-Glass*, op. cit., pp. 27–31.]

20 The only book to pose this question, to take the history of medicine as one example, seems, as far as we know, to be that of Cruchet, *De la méthode de la médecine*, Paris: PUF.

21* Translators' note: the French word *régime* can be translated as 'diet' as well as 'regime'.

22 Nathalie Sarraute, *L'Ere du soupçon*, Paris: Gallimard, 1964, p. 52.

Chapter 4

1 Kleist, *On the Marionette Theatre*.
2 Scott Fitzgerald, op. cit.
3 S. A. Kierkegaard, *Fear and Trembling*, trans. Walter Lowrie, Princeton: Princeton University Press, 1968 (and the way in which Kierkegaard,

in relation to movement, sketches a series of scripts which already
belong to the cinema).

4   Fernand Deligny, 'Cahiers de l'immuable', *Recherches* no. 18, Paris:
     Recherches, 1975.

5   Pierrette Fleutiaux, *Histoire du gouffre et de la lunette*, Paris: Julliard, 1976.

6   Paul Virilio, *Essai sur l'insécurité du territoire*, Paris: Stock, 1976.

7   Georges Dumézil, *Heur et malheur du geurrier*, Paris: PUF, 1969; and *Mythe et
     Epopée*, Volume II, Paris: Gallimard, 1971. Luc du Heusch, *Le roi ivre ou
     l'origine de l'Etat*, Paris: Gallimard.

8   Pierre Clastres, 'La Guerre dans les sociétés, *Libre*, no. 1, Paris: Payot.

9   On all these points cf. Félix Guattari, 'La Grande Illusion', in *Le Monde*.

Chapter 5

1*   Translator's note: The reader familiar with Deleuze's work cannot
     help but be struck by something odd, something disquieting, in the
     French text of 'L'actuel et la virtuel'. The anomalous nature of the
     piece is most evident on the stylistic plane, for unlike most of
     Deleuze's writing, in which a thought of soaring complexity is
     expressed with an elegant, limpid clarity, 'L'actuel' is composed of a
     series of jarringly repetitive monophrasal sentences. Sentences which
     are frequently blunt assertions of the form 'the virtual is x' rather
     than Deleuze's customary rigorous philosophical argumentation. My
     personal suspicion, and the only way to satisfactorily account for the
     oddity of the text, is that, rather than a finished paper, 'L'actuel et la
     virtuel' is a series of notes, drafts, or *aides-mémoires* for a paper.
     Neither the French edition nor the Italian translation (the two
     editions that I have seen of the text) voices any of these concerns;
     however, when I raised my reservations about the text with Eric
     Alliez, one of the most perceptive of Deleuze's readers, he replied
     that it is 'quite obvious' that 'L'actuel et la virtuel' is a draft.

2*   Translator's note: Both Caroline Warman and Matteo Mandarini
     made insightful comments on early versions of this translation,
     comments which no doubt improved it immeasurably and for which I
     thank them.

3*   Translator's note: Cf. Gilles Deleuze, *Différence et répétition* (Vendome:
     Presses Universitaires de France, 1968), trans. by Paul Patton as
     Difference and Repetition (London: Athlone Press, 1994), pp. 270–1/
     209: 'Every object is double without it being the case that the two
     halves resemble one another, one being a virtual image and the
     other an actual image.'

4   Michel Cassé, *Du vide et de la création* (Paris: Éditions Odile Jacob),
     pp. 72–3. See also Pierre Lévy's study, *Qu'est-ce que la virtuel?* (Paris:
     Éditions de la Découverte).

5   Henri Bergson, *Matière et la memoire* (Paris: Éditions du centenaire), trans. by N. M. Paul and W. S. Palmer as *Matter and Memory* (New York: Zone Books, 1991), p. 250/104; chapters II and III analyse the virtuality of memory and its actualization. [Translator's note: It is worth noting that these chapters also contain the elaboration of the interlinked concepts of the circuits of memory, contraction and expansion, the coexistence of past with the present, that provide the basis for Bergson's utterly non-psychologizing account of memory, as well as the opening, and indeed ever-present, structure of the present article. The concept of the circuit is introduced by Bergson as an explicit challenge to, and attack upon, the then-dominant accounts of memory in the following way: 'There is supposed to be a rectilinear progress, by which the mind goes further and further from the object, never to return to it. We maintain, on the contrary, that reflective perception is a *circuit*, in which all the elements, including the perceived object itself, hold each other in a state of mutual tension' (p. 250/104).]

6   See Gilles Châtelet, *Les Enjeux du mobile* (Paris: Éditions du Seuil), pp. 54–68 (from 'virtual speeds' to 'virtual cuts').

7* Translator's note: This 'inner circuit' is what Bergson describes as the 'moment when the recollection ... is capable of blending so well with the present perception that we cannot say where perception ends or where memory begins' (*Matter and Memory*, p. 106).

8   Henri Bergson, *L'Énergie spirituelle*, 'memory of the present', pp. 917–20. Bergson insists on two movements, that towards larger and larger circles, and that towards a narrower and narrower circle. [Translator's note: *Mind-Energy*, trans. by H. Wildon Carr (London: Macmillan, 1920), pp. 134–7. Bergson writes: 'Memory seems to be to the perception what the image reflected in the mirror is to the object in front of it. The object can be touched as well as seen; acts on us as well as we on it; is pregnant with possible actions; it is *actual*' (p. 134).]

9   The discipline of optics takes the actual object and the virtual image as its starting-points and shows in what circumstances that object becomes virtual, that image actual, and then how both object and image become either actual or virtual.

10* Translator's note: Deleuze had referred to this split, inherited from Bergson, earlier in his work, perhaps most notably in his exposition of crystal time in *Cinema 2: The Time-Image*, trans. by Hugh Tomlinson and Robert Galeta (London: The Athlone Press, 1989), where he writes of time splitting into 'two dissymmetrical jets, one of which makes all the present pass on, while the other preserves all the past'

(p. 81). One can go further and suggest that, as Deleuze notes above, much of the conceptual basis for the present piece is derived from the section on the 'memory of the present' in Bergson's *L'Énergie spirituelle*, and that a great deal of it had already been extensively developed and deployed in the above-mentioned chapter of *Cinema 2*. It is worth remembering as a subject for further investigation that Walter Benjamin – whose admiration for Bergonson is well known but, as yet, inadequately explored – had, in an important passage in his *Arcades Project* (Cambridge, MA: Harvard University Press, 1999), referred to 'the crystal of the total event' (N2, 6).

Chapter 6

We would like to thank Anne-Lise Feral and Matthew McGuire for their invaluable advice.

1. Both *pouvoir* and *puissance* are usually translated as 'power', but because Deleuze and Châtelet draw a clear distinction between the two and because the two words are used too closely together to gracefully clarify the meaning in parentheses, in what follows we have translated *puissance* as 'potential' and *pouvoir* as 'power'. See Martin Joughin's note in his translation of Deleuze's *Expressionism and Philosophy*, p. 407n; see p. 93 of the same book for the relation between power and act. It should also be noted that although we translate 'l'acte' as 'the act' it can also be read as 'actuality'.

2. Cf. *The Logic of Sense*, p. 154.

Index

European Perspectives

A Series in Social Thought and Cultural Criticism

Lawrence D. Kritzman, Editor

Claudia Benthien	*Skin: On the Cultural Border Between Self and the World*
Emmanuel Todd	*After the Empire: The Breakdown of the American Order*
Gianni Vattimo	*Nihilism and Emancipation: Ethics, Politics, and Law*
Julia Kristeva	*Colette*
Steve Redhead, ed.	*The Paul Virilio Reader*
Roland Barthes	*The Neutral: Lecture Course at the Collège de France (1977–1978)*
Gianni Vattimo	*Dialogue with Nietzsche*
Gilles Deleuze	*Nietzsche and Philosophy*
Hélène Cixous	*Dream I Tell You*
Jacques Derrida	*Geneses, Genealogies, Genres, and Genius: The Secrets of the Archive*